The Capitalist Manifesto

Dimitriy N. Mishin

Contents

Introduction & Special Thanks.

Dear Reader,

It is my great pleasure to connect with you through my work. I thank you for committing to read the Manifesto and truly hope this book can have a transformative impact on your life – its contents certainly have the potential to do so.

First and foremost, allow me to establish my own credibility in your eyes and answer the rightful question: "Who the hell am I to teach you anything about wealth?". Is this not another "Get Rich Quick" manual written by a nobody that's achieved nothing? Today, thanks to the abundance of "Rich Kid" Instagram posts, rented Lamborghinis, and fake "gurus," the status of a self-made millionaire has been somewhat devalued. People have seen a lot and are no longer that impressed or interested; I will therefore not ramble on about how I generated hundreds of thousands of dollars in portfolio returns, recognized unique investment opportunities (one such was buying Bitcoin at $2500 and selling at $16,000), started three businesses, and employed impressive capital all by the age of 19. I will not flood you with empty promises or entertain the illusion that, having read the "Manifesto," you will become an overnight millionaire. My personal successes are a product of a formulaic process of carefully following a certain set of principles and ideas. That set of principles and ideas is very much quantifiable and transferrable, and in the "Capitalist Manifesto," I quantify and transfer them.

Aside from being someone with rich experiences of their own, I'm also a guy that has read a lot of self-development and business books –some of the lessons I've learned from those are just as crucial as those sourced in my personal practices. You see, as I've indulged in my quest for knowledge about wealth, money, success, and self-realization, I quickly came to discover one simple truth: these books are all essentially talking about the same things. Of course, there is significant deviation between some, and to say that each single one of them is not worth reading would be a crude oversimplification. However, there are a few recurring commonalities one spots as he reads more and more of such literature. This is because various paths to success may differ in form, but most are similar in substance.

Why am I selling you this? Shouldn't I spread the knowledge free of charge and enable others' financial gain akin to mine? Well, first and foremost – where there is easy money to be made, I go out and make it. Only a madman would do otherwise. Ray Dalio's "Principles" (a great book!) cost me $12.50, and I'm sure that my purchase hasn't had too profound of an impact on his 20-billion-dollar fortune. Yet even he, who could easily afford to publish his book at a loss, has not made it free. Your monetary commitment shows your dedication to reading this – and this, to me, is of far greater importance than your money. I want to know that my work has changed lives of those who've read it – even just a little bit. At the end of the day, conveying valuable information to my readers is my main motivation behind writing the Manifesto because I will still do well if this book doesn't sell, but some of you might not.

This is the Capitalist Manifesto. This is my best attempt at extracting the utmost value from the hundreds of lessons I have myself learned and from the hundreds of books I've read and condensing it into one quintessential document. Consider this, above all, a time-saving book: I've done the work for you and now I share with you the most crucial knowledge that I have acquired. But keep in mind: this script is biased and full of personal views. What I consider of superior importance may be deemed trivial by others. My use of personal examples here is more plentiful than the allusions to the books I've read – therefore, care not to consider this a mere academic summary. Instead, try to trust and allow this book to change your day to day life – to whatever extent you deem plausible.

When reading the Manifesto, be prepared to stumble into terms and phrases you are not familiar with. To reap the greatest possible benefit from my writing, approach the book proactively – Google things you don't understand, highlight key ideas, complete the suggested exercises and try reading further about the concepts that interest you. The Manifesto is not a novel - it is a cluster of knowledge. Revisiting ideas and re-reading pages are no waste of time!

Being an author is far from what I envision of my future and this may well be the only book I'll ever write. With that said, I promise to continue dispensing valuable information through other means of communication available to me. Your feedback is important, your questions are valuable, your correspondence is consequential. I will leave all my details in the epilogue – please do not hesitate to reach out!

I have given you all I could at this point in time. Some people will read the Manifesto thoroughly and change their lives for the better, while some others may not even finish it. I've caught the "Golden Snitch" for you and am holding it in the palm of my hand. Will you reach out and snatch it? That, my friends, is at your sole discretion.

Warmly Yours,

Dimitriy N. Mishin

Special Thanks:

To all the people without whom I wouldn't be the man I am today and without whom the "Manifesto" wouldn't be the "Manifesto:"

- *Nikita Mishin & Kseniya Rubina (my dear father and mother)*
- *Feodor Mishin & The Mishin-Rubin Clan*
- *Konstantin Nikolaev, Andrey Filatov*
- *Alexander Guselnikov*
- *Arseniy Zibarev, Dominik Ramanuskas, Dmitry Markov*
- *Maria Drokova, Evan Luthra, Daria Ratobylskaya*
- *Ray Dalio, Peter Thiel, George Clason.*
- *Nathaniel Gerdes & The Team*
- *Ivan Mast, Roscoe Marshall, Stephan Ellis, Charles Sin, Matteo Loria, Noah Rigg & others*

Thank you.

Chapter 1:

The Fundamentals

Jim Carrey – a world-renowned comedian – and, in my opinion, one of the greatest comedic artists still living, once told the story of his father – Percy Joseph Carrey. Percy's story is much gloomier than that of his son – his early-on failure to succeed as a musician and comedian had led him to abandon his dreams and go for a "safe" job as an accountant. Percy had a family to feed and slaved himself for an employer that would, as soon as necessary, let him go and would not think twice. In fact, this is exactly what happened. The 1979 Oil Shock sent the economy into turbulence, and Percy was fecklessly let go from that very "safe and stable" job he had been killing himself for. The Carreys were living on the streets.

Then, crafted through financial difficulty and tempered by rocky times, out came Jim, and he wasn't going to repeat his father's fatal mistake. Jim learned the hard way: *"you can fail at what you don't like, so you might as well try doing what you love."* Look at Jim now.

So, what has this story got to do with the "Capitalist Manifesto?" Well, everything. Before we even begin treading the path of financial instruments, passive income, spending habits and more, you must pose these questions to yourself: "Am I doing what I do for me or am I doing it for someone (or something) else? Am I a slave of circumstance? Am I attending university to please my parents and fit the status quo? Am I working a tedious 9 to 5 just to pay off my debt? Am I sacrificing my life's passion for "safety" and perceived financial stability?" If the answer to any of these questions is "yes," don't worry – most people living in this world are in a similar position. The most important thing you can do now is *acknowledge* the fact that you aren't doing what you love. When you do this, you may begin thinking about what it is you might do instead *if* you had the money, time or whatever else. It's okay not to know what your passion or so-called "destiny" is (though I believe there is no such thing), but it's crucial to know what it's *not*. Once you have made this clear in your own mind, you can proceed to consider how exactly you will go about achieving financial freedom, which in turn will grant you a broader freedom to do what you love. Money can't buy happiness, but it can buy you control of your own time and *that* can get you as close as you may be. As some clever man once said: "Money sure does not buy happiness, but I'd much rather cry in my Mercedes than on my bike."

Does money work for you or do you work for money?

I despise using clichés because I always feel like there are better expressions for my thought, but this snazzy little saying really does form the basis of financial freedom. This concept is crucial to extracting the greatest possible gain from this book and if I were to summarize it in one sentence it would sound something like this: all people in this world can be placed on a broad spectrum, at the extremes of which are - **money slaves and money masters.**

Money slaves take a *passive* approach to their financial affairs and are consequently *subjects* of the money system. They typically receive a salary and have little or no assets, spending their hard-earned cash on liabilities (things that lose value and take money *out* of your pocket) such as cars, luxury clothes, or (worst of all) debt. Money masters, on the other hand, take on a more *active* approach and thus *subjugate* the money system, reaping reward in the form of profits. They almost always have several income streams generated by assets (things that gain value and put money *into* your pocket) such as stocks, real estate, or other miscellaneous investments. It is crucial to understand the difference between the two and be honest with yourself when classing yourself and your possessions as one or the other. If you go and buy a new house which you do not plan to lease out or sell in the nearest future, it is a liability. If you go and buy a Rolex watch, it is a liability. If you're using a credit card, this is also a liability. *"Rich Dad Poor Dad"* does an excellent job in explaining the difference between the two. So, if you seek more detail on assets and liabilities, by all means, do invest in Kiyosaki's book.

Picture a hard-working state school literature teacher named Curtis. Curtis has a family of five, which he dearly loves spending time with (having completed his nine-hour daily shifts). He barely makes ends meet – he spends all of his $2500 monthly income on rent, food, and clothes. Curtis may be a nice guy, but he exemplifies a *money slave* – he works for money and money does not work for him.

Now picture Jeff, who is a whole different kind of folk – he works at an investment bank on Wall Street. His salary is at the lower end of the six-figure range, and yet his personal net worth is comfortably in the millions. Jeff makes more from his investments than he does from his job (which theoretically should be his main income stream). Specifically, Jeff hosts three small Airbnb properties in Manhattan, invests in Emerging Market bonds, and owns a thick stash of AT&T stock which pay him generous dividends annually. Jeff is a *money master* – he organized his finance in such a way that his job is no longer his primary income source. Jeff made his money work *for* him.

You might say: "These two people most probably came from two very different backgrounds, and opportunities available to Jeff were never there for Curtis." While there is minor truth to that, you'd probably be surprised to learn that Curtis and Jeff share a lot in common, not least of which is their surname. Curtis and Jeff are brothers – born into the very same lower-middle-class family just six years apart. Not only that, they also went to the same high school and graduated from the same university. The current difference in their financial status is primarily explained by different choices made by each brother at various points in their lives. Curtis subconsciously (not without a "guiding" hand from his strict father) defined success as academic merit. From a young age, he focused heavily on *theory-rich* literary study and proudly left college with an "English Language" degree. Jeff, on the other hand, saw college merely as a viable opportunity to acquire *practical knowledge, experience, and acquaintances in* the field of economics and finance. He did not care about graduating with the highest honours possible, instead, he used his time at university to build a solid foundation for his goal – financial attainment.

We have just briefly examined two very different life paths of two people that started off in the exact same place. One made his parents proud with his "Ivy-League-esque" academic excellence yet failed to find a practical use for his knowledge and had, therefore, settle for (let's be honest) a pretty meagre wage of a state schoolteacher. The other paid far greater attention to the numbers in his bank account than the letters on his graduation certificate. He may be no scholar, but he's far better off financially. The two examples are extremes but go to underline an important point: the vast majority of people should see college as an investment above all. Furthermore, in order to be in a good financial position, one must start thinking about their finances early (or think about them circumstantially and accept financial struggles as a trade-off).

As a brief postscript: there is nothing wrong with academic excellence nor am I implying all university courses should be chosen with *vocational* training in mind. If you have the luxury of being able to choose a degree based solely on what you find interesting, or because you strive to exceed academically, by all means, feel free to do so. My point is that far too many people are being trivial about choices they make in university and do not associate them closely enough with their future financial position.

So, the lessons to be learned:

1. *If you aren't living how you want, acknowledge it. Then think about changing things in your life.*

   There really isn't much more to say here. Coming to clear terms with your current position in life and setting a goal of where you want to be is important for successful application of the "Capitalist Manifesto." If you don't have a goal which you strive to achieve with burning passion, you will run out of energy long before you'll finish sowing the seeds of your financial advancement crops.

2. *A degree has almost nothing to do with financial freedom and everything to do with what you make of it.*

Curtis, by a mile, is not alone in the group of mildly disappointed, "still-hoping-for-something-better" ladies and gentlemen who went to the best universities in the world yet are confusedly waiting for a job of a similar level. Likewise, Jeff is not the only cunning little man who simply made money a priority and acted in accord with his goal – making the most of his college years (which didn't necessarily involve studying hard for hours straight like his big brother). You can go to NYU and be far more successful than your pal who went to Harvard. It's about your goal and about your head, not your college degree.

3. *You don't choose where you start, but it's entirely down to you where you end up. Anyone can "make it" (but relatively few will).*

Leaving Curtis and Jeff aside for a while, there are countless examples of well-known billionaires that started off with nothing. Take Jack Ma (Alibaba founder) as your first example – the man didn't even get a job at KFC when he first applied and was rejected from Harvard nine times. Mr Ma, by the way, is now worth more than 40 billion dollars. As calming as it is to blame billionaires' success on luck and circumstance, this isn't going to cut it. Face it: if you are born poor it's not your fault, but if you die poor it arguably is.

4. *If you want to be a money master, consider reducing your exposure to liabilities and building up your assets.*

You may *want* some things, but you probably don't *need* them. Here's a thought: instead of taking out a loan and putting your own capital in chains for years ahead, don't buy that car. Don't go out for that dinner. Don't buy that handbag. Restrain yourself and reap the benefits. "So, what DO I buy?!" – all you've got to do is keep on reading!

Chapter 2:

Your Most Important Asset

Whatever your life situation is, the fact that you're reading this book suggests you are seeking change to your current financial position. Hopefully, having read the first chapter, you've chosen to become a better **money master**. In chapters 3, 4, and 5, I will talk about the various strategies available to all kinds of people – from a college student to an office employee. But just before you proceed to identify yourself as a "Money Newbie" or a "Finance Hardo," I'm going to draw your attention to one universal truth:

Your most important asset is your mind.

I honestly cannot stress this enough. The best investments I've made during my life are not stocks, funds, or private equity, nor did they cost me millions of dollars. The best investments were ones made into my head and often, they actually come to me for free. It cost me nothing to download "Business Insider" and "Yahoo Finance" on my phone and some of the best business and finance books I've read only set me back 20 or 30 bucks. A return, though, is guaranteed, and the premium offered to the buyer is incomparably disproportional to the couple of hours you spend reading a quality book (or, for that matter, the two or three Starbucks Latte's you gave up to buy it in the first place). Each day, you're awake for roughly 16 hours – use that time wisely and suffocate time-wasting habits like Instagram, Facebook or (non-educational) YouTube. *Knowledge is power. Do everything you can to educate yourself.*

Now, it may well seem to some that what I've said above goes against my scepticism over Curtis' sheepish grin for the best education possible outlined in Chapter 1. Not exactly. First and foremost, the self-education I talk about in this chapter is most often not the same as university education. Furthermore, occasionally, the two are polar opposites! It may be much more useful for me to go to the TechCrunch conference in San Francisco, and yet here I am, sitting in a freezing cold auditorium learning about matrices and integration. To briefly re-visit our poor old Curtis – he, unfortunately, (despite being a clever student) was not being smart about his education. He did English Language at college because his father thought it would be an impressive degree to have. Or, perhaps, because he found it slightly easier than any other subject. Or maybe it was because his best friend chose to do it, hence Curtis followed. Regardless, Curtis' college education ended up being quite narrowly (and too deeply) concentrated on English Language. Even more importantly, it was never aligned with a broader target that Curtis should have set himself like his younger brother. It was a monotonous, tiring process of swallowing force-fed information without questioning of its purpose by the recipient. Curtis would have been much better off skipping his morning lectures and reading "The Times." Sadly, he was caught up in the indoctrinating conveyor belt of the flawed university education system.

So, how exactly do you educate yourself? There is an infinite number of things in this world you could (and should) know and there is a very finite amount of time you have at your disposal to try to get to know them. It can be very overwhelming. The first step in self-education is to be **generally knowledgeable**. You really never know when your general knowledge can come in handy. From personal experience, some of the knowledge I've picked up in most random situations (knowledge which has absolutely nothing to do with my field of study or work) has literally been life-changing.

One time, I was at a big charity ball event co-sponsored by our family friend. I've heard two foreign gentlemen (both about 8 years older than me) entering a mildly heated argument about which mythological God was the patron of war. The smaller, blonde man was vehemently asserting it was Mars. The taller man, less confidently, persisted it was Ares. I just happened to have remembered from a book I've read at 12 years old that the two were just different Greek and Roman names for the same God. I walked across to their table. "Gentlemen," I said, "I'm sorry to intrude, but you are both right." Upon brief explanation, both said: "Hmmm," in unison. I was immediately invited to join their table and we got talking. I left the reception with a new friend and (as I later discovered) the telephone number of a big European VC fund manager. Years down the line, we're still great buddies and have successfully executed two excellent private equity deals. I would have never thought knowing the difference (or, rather, lack thereof) between Mars and Ares would quite literally make me money... What I know for sure is this: had I not known that difference, I would have never made that acquaintance.

I have had several similar occasions where random general knowledge has helped me get ahead in life. I'm not asking you to go learn the Greek mythology from A to Z, but I want you to know that often the information you dismiss as irrelevant may prove incredibly useful. Knowing a lot not only makes you an interesting dinner table conversationalist (and an attractive male in the eyes of less knowledgeable female counterparts), it also opens the most unexpected and wonderful doors.

Moving onto the specifics of how to acquire this general knowledge: *READ*. You probably know that the average CEO reads 60 books per year. Warren Buffet, for instance, reads 600-1000 pages each day (which is insane). Read books – be it novels, autobiographies or finance. Read newspapers and stay up to date on global issues. R.E.A.D! Even if it's only 20 minutes each day – that's far better than 20 minutes of meaningless Instagram Feed scrolling. Did you know that Gold Prices have hit a five-year low? What about the Trump – Xi trade war developments? Are you aware that the US just killed the highest-ranking Iranian army general on Iraqi soil? Do you even believe in Global Warming? By reading up on all these things, you also enable yourself to form an opinion and that makes you a much more sophisticated and unconventional individual. Besides, you never know, someone important may agree with you at the right place and at the right time. The Annex of "Capitalist Manifesto" lists almost all the news sources I follow alongside with a recommended fiction & non-fiction reading list. I do recommend you have a browse and pick a few things up – this should give you a solid kickstart to building up your general knowledge.

Then, be *specifically knowledgeable.* This will make more sense and is better put into context in the next few chapters where we move on to discuss the types of assets which you, depending on circumstance specific to your reality, should own. Regardless of whether it's going to be real estate or high-risk growth stocks, you will need to educate yourself to handle your asset in the most effective way possible. Information in our day and age is as accessible as ever. There is no limit to what you can know. The more information you have about your holdings, your market, and potential influences on the value of your assets, the better your decisions can be.

For example, let's say you own shares in a Canadian e-commerce company called Shopify. $SHOP is a relatively volatile, moderately risky growth stock. You intend to hold it for several years.

Firstly, you are Shopify's shareholder. You need to have a clear understanding about its business model. Watch out for the quarterly reports – how do they affect the share price? It's best to choose a few metrics by which you can judge your company's performance. Have year on year profits been increasing? Has revenue growth been slowing or accelerating? Is the company's CEO doing an adequate job in tackling scaling issues? What are the expansion plans? Has the company run out of steam or does it still have a way to go up? Knowing the answers to these questions is essential. Perhaps, some of those answers will make you swap Shopify for another, better company which has a competitive edge. Either way, you're much better off just having Shopify in your portfolio than 12 stocks you know close to nothing about.

Secondly, you are a stakeholder in the digital economy. You need to maintain an awareness about the broader industry and use different cues to make investment decisions. Know the big players in the market. To come back to our Shopify example: how related (or threatened) is Shopify's success to Amazon's tyrannous dominance of e-commerce? Perhaps, Amazon's recent acquisition of Whole

Foods suggests Shopify's niche remains untouched. Or maybe, Amazon is planning to focus on creating a more intuitive sales platform and its huge economies of scale will trump Shopify's business & sink the stock price? Similarly, what about EU's GDPR regulations? Does this create trouble for Shopify and impair its business model? If you don't read up on your industry, you'll never know, and if you'll never know, you will lose money.

Lastly, you are a participant of the US stock market and hence, the value of your asset and the state of your industry is subject to greater forces beyond your field of direct interest. The Trump trade war affects the stock market, and if yet another trade negotiation has been flunked, the value of your Shopify holdings will tank regardless of how well Shopify itself is doing. The inverted yield curve (in the past a relatively accurate indicator forecasting recessions), once again, will have an adverse impact on your asset – investors will sell out of fear, disregarding the booming state of e-commerce industry. Be aware of the broader global events and make sure to differentiate between which of those do (or don't) cause changes in the prices of your stock – for instance, unlike the yield curve, a sharp fall in silver prices will likely have limited impact on Shopify's shares.

I don't want my use of Shopify stock above as an example of how to be *specifically knowledgeable* to throw people off. It may contain several unfamiliar terms or references which many readers might not understand. That's okay! Firstly, you can learn more and look things up. But secondly, and more importantly, this approach is broadly applicable with whatever asset you may chose. Here, I try to illustrate the comprehensive method with which you should assess your holdings – the method which forms a basis for making decisions on when (or what) to sell or buy, for instance. Lastly, don't be afraid to have an opinion (this, by the way, does not necessarily mean you should always express it). This applies both to general and specific knowledge – the knowledge you obtain, you can (and should) use. If you think, for instance, that Trump's attitude towards the American trade deficit with China is, in fact, appropriate, don't be afraid to say it. So long as you justify your opinion, first to yourself and then to others, it is valid. Besides, you might be surprised about how many business people actually approve of Mr Trump's policy towards China.

Having an opinion when buying assets is also critical – if you can't choose to believe in one company over another, or buy real estate in a specific neighbourhood instead of the one next door, you will be forever stuck trying to sit one bottom on two chairs. That said, make your opinion as objective and unbiased as possible. Revisit and re-justify it and use your conclusions as motives for your investments.

Synergize the two types of knowledge. Often times, they complement each other in surprising and pleasant ways! Remember, general knowledge will make you friends and specific knowledge will make you money.

Chapter 3:

Enslaving Money

Bearing in mind what you have learned about the value of self-education, the question looms: now what? How exactly does one become a **money master**? Acquiring knowledge, both general and specific, is an infinite process, an ideal which we should all strive towards and is just the first, among many, step in your journey. Just being knowledgeable won't magically add zeros to your bank account. This chapter will focus on the specifics of the first actions you could take to become a true money master with multiple income streams.

"The Richest Man in Babylon" by George Clason is an excellent book. It is, quite simply, about the richest man in Babylon - a Mesopotamian superpower that existed from 18th to 6th century AD – many historians today consider Babylon to have been the wealthiest city in human history. The man's name was Arkad – his life story is that of a slave who came from rags to riches. Clason, through Arkad's mouth, creates a clever allegory to illustrate the mentality behind his success: *treat money as your children.* Children who will work for you and give you grandchildren that will also work for you, who will, in turn, give you great-grandchildren that will do the same. This way, you will end up with an ever-growing family all of which works for you. Though having children in modern-day and age for the sole

purpose of their labour is a little inappropriate, this Babylonian principle is still very much applicable to your perception of your money.

To employ the simplest example. Let's say you suddenly find yourself with a spare 1000 dollars lying around. You can spend that thousand on a liability, like a handbag or some new clothes, and this, in Babylonian terms, is equivalent to killing your child. This thousand – your beloved son – can no longer work for you, nor can it reproduce and bring you children that will also work for you. Alternatively, you can lend that thousand to an acquaintance in need and charge an interest rate of 10% per annum. You'll temporarily miss out on the handbag, but in a year's time, you will have $1100. Subtract the thousand you started with and you're left with $100. Say hello to your grandchild! This $100 is a product of the $1000 you began with, and now this hundred can also work for you.

Now, let's make things a little more real: no one randomly finds one thousand dollars. Not everyone has a neighbour that needs money and not every neighbour will accept an interest rate of 10% per annum. This is why you need to work with what you have to "conceive" your first child and to explain this, we revisit the story of Arkad.

Arkad began his journey to wealth with no money in his pocket and some invaluable advice from a wise man: *take 10% of what you make and set it aside*. To Arkad, who was paid very little by his brutish master, living on 10% less seemed impossible at first. *"I will starve,"* he thought to himself. *"My clothes will get raggedy and I won't be drinking any wine."* Yet, to his great surprise, having 10% less food on his plate had no adverse impact on his health. His clothes, though replaced less often, were very much fit for purpose, and as for the wine – he felt much fresher on Monday mornings. After six months of setting aside 10% of his miserable salary, Arkad was ready to invest. Or so he thought…

In search for a profitable venture, Arkad stumbled across a pottery maker, who offered Arkad the "opportunity of his lifetime." The potter was on his way to Palestine, where precious jewels and gemstones were being sold at a bargain price. The plan was to return to Babylon three months later and sell the stones with pleasing profit. Arkad didn't think long – *"This,"* he thought, *"will make me a richer man."* He gave his savings to the potter.

Six months passed, and the potter still had not made himself known. On the seventh month, the potter returned and, to Arkad's detriment, confessed that the jewels he was sold in Palestine were, in fact, worthless pieces of coloured glass and could not be resold in Babylon. Arkad lost all of his savings.

Perhaps, if he could have read "The Capitalist Manifesto," his *general knowledge* would have allowed him to suspect a potter is not the best candidate to be entrusted with jewel trading, while his *specific knowledge* would allow him to travel to Palestine himself and differentiate real jewels from worthless pieces of tinted glass. Sadly, Arkad never read "The Capitalist Manifesto," but he did remember the advice once given to him by a wise man. He did not let his failure put him off from saving up and trying again.

I will refrain from re-telling the story of Arkad in its entirety – if you found it interesting, you should definitely buy Clason's book. In short: Arkad saved up several times, failed in choosing the right investments several times, and lost money several times. This process was a costly one for Arkad in terms of his golden coins, but it also granted him with invaluable "coins" of experience. Once enough of such coins have been accumulated, their weight had become substantial enough to tip the weight of the scales – Arkad has made his first successful investment; and then the second; and the third. He was diligent and reinvested any profit that he made. Then eventually, by following this simple strategy, Arkad became the richest man in Babylon.

From a personal perspective, I find this story truly relatable because it accurately resembles how I got into stock trading. I was a 13-year-old boarding school student at the time, and all the older boys I hanged out with used to do stocks. I wanted to do it too. I watched a couple of YouTube videos, made a trading simulator account, and even read a book (most of which I did not understand at the time). I was so sure I was ready. I went "all-in" with my 400-dollar savings and lost it all. It was a devastating blow to my ego and my pocket, but, just like the 21-st century Arkad, I never gave up. I tried again and failed again. I repeated this painful and expensive cycle five times before I made my first victorious profit of $24.89. Which I, of course, re-invested.

Hopefully, the story of Arkad coupled with my own experience give you a *broad* idea about how to invest (and re-invest). But what do you invest in? How do you start off with stocks? Or cryptocurrency? Or real estate? When people ask me these questions online, I revert with three questions of my own:

1. *How soon do you want a return on your money?*

2. *How much time are you willing to spend working for that money?*

3. *How much risk are you willing to take on to make that money?*

The answers to these questions will determine your investment strategy. It is *crucial* for you to know the answers and to use them to guide your choice of assets for the next chapters. It's also important to be realistic about how much money you are prepared to set aside and invest. If we're working with $5,000, real estate is not really an option for you at this time. Be objective.

If you are a "rich-daddy-nice-mommy" Regents University student who doesn't mind-blowing large sums – consider a high-risk investment like Bitcoin a viable option. If, on the other hand, you are a single mother working three jobs and barely making ends meet, you should probably steer well clear of Bitcoin and accept lower potential returns as a trade-off for asset stability. You might be better off investing in conservative dividend stocks – they won't deliver thousands of percent in returns, but they will offer relative security and consistent passive income. Similarly, if you're looking for a return within a three-month period, you're most probably not going for private equity – returns here most often take years or even decades. I can go on and on with these examples, but I will leave it up to you to think of answers to my three questions and use the information about each asset type in the next chapters to make the best decisions.

A few more summative "Manifesto points" before moving onto asset types:

- *Reduce your expenses and use the liberated cash to start investing.*

As much as I don't want to make this book prescriptive, there are some simple certitudes no one can get around. This is one of them – if you want change to your financial position, you have to start with something. Some of my readers will be lucky enough to have free capital at their disposal and to them, this rule is less applicable. Many readers, though, will find themselves in a different situation whereby their pay-check-to-paycheck routines, their student lifestyle or bloated expense habits leave them no other choice than to reduce ex-penses in order to find initial capital for investment. This isn't too comfortable but has to be done.

- *As a rule of thumb, don't overcomplicate, overdo or overthink your investments.*

It is far better to have three or four assets that you understand well and that feed you good than to own 50 different stocks, derivatives, cryptocurrencies, or commodities you under-stand very little about. Those three or four assets, if chosen well, will deliver great returns, and great returns are better than mediocre ones (and even more so than losses!).

- *Do not be scared of losing money when investing! But make sure to learn from it...*

I'm not Gary Vee and so I'm not going to demonstratively recommend you "eat shit" or "lose money" on purpose. How-ever, while not-too-poor and not-so-old Gary does make lu-dicrous statements for attention, our Instagram fellow does have a fair point as the foundation for his claims. In short, be like Arkad. If he hadn't given his money to the potter, and subsequently failed multiple times over, he would have never gained the "coins of experience" which later allowed him to make successful investment decisions. As unpleasant as it gets, it is occasionally useful to lose money so long as you always ask yourself what you did wrong and what you can improve. Implement the experience you obtain when failing, and you will succeed.

Chapter 4:

Basic Securities

I want to reinforce the nature of the next two chapters: I will not be doing any spoon-feeding. I will not tell you which companies to buy, what bonds have the highest yields, what cryptocurrency is legitimate, and which is a fad, nor which city is currently best to do real estate. The examples I employ are not investment recommendations nor are they necessarily assets I own. My aim is to provide you with a menu of "dishes" that you can pick and choose from - each dish will be described in varying amounts of detail and will be recommended to people with varied "dietary requirements." Please do not approach these chapters with a "copy-paste" attitude, instead, use the information as a stepping-stone to build your own knowledge and then your own assets.

Hopefully, by either reducing your expenses, restructuring their composition or using auxiliary cash you have handy, you'll manage to produce an amount of money you're ready to invest. Chapters 4 and 5 will focus on our asset types – the securities (both basic and non-basic). It is worth mentioning now that some asset types outlined in the next chapter are strictly speaking not securities, but we refer to them as such for the purpose of convenience.

Securities are any tradeable financial asset and include stocks, bonds, and derivatives amongst other financial instruments. Before such terms discourage any amateur readers, I must say: if you do not know what "bonds" or "derivatives" are, don't worry. Once we get to it, you will understand that a lot of these things are actually relatively simple and are guided by common sense. Wall Street makes things out to be substantially more difficult than they are, by labelling them with long names and scary-sounding abbreviations. Relax and let me take you through this.

Quite frankly, I struggle to think of any reader profile who should avoid securities altogether – in other words, *you* will most certainly need securities to make yourself more money. Employing the tools outlined in my "Securities" chapters is your most realistic shot at becoming wealthier, so consider paying close attention.

The ultimate aim for you is to use the information provided in the next few chapters to comprise your own security portfolio – a "wish list" of stocks, bonds, and other financial instruments. You can then proceed to visit your bank, contact a broker or find an online platform for buying, storing, and selling these securities. I will mention specific tools available to you in the annex.

The elephant in the room is the Stock Market. This beast made people billion-dollar fortunes and wiped them out just as rapidly. Everyone knows about it – some people hate it, others love it, but most don't even try to understand it. People don't understand why it goes up or down, why some stocks are worth thousands of dollars while others are worth pennies, why the 1929 and 2008 crises occurred, and why the losses in the stock market translate into salary cuts. Broadly speaking, people consider the Stock Market to be risky and speculative – a dangerous, unfamiliar machine which is easier to ignore than to attempt to operate. In reality, it is no more than a manmade mechanism that facilitates wealth transfers. From the impatient to the patient, from the hot-headed to the calm, from the careless to the diligent, and so on.

It's worth mentioning that while there are multiple different stock markets in several countries (Hong-Kong, China, Russia, Japan, UK, and more), I would expect most readers to focus in on the US – specifically, the New York Stock Exchange. Not only is it the world's biggest stock exchange with over 25 trillion dollars in capitalization, it's also one of the most popular and varied (with over 2400 companies listed, many of which are international). For stock market amateurs, I would suggest NYSE as the go-to for first experience.

The stock market is universal in its accessibility and diversity. It can make you money sooner or later, a lot or a little, and it can be extremely risky or barely risky at all. Regardless of who you are, you can take advantage of it. There are multiple investment strategies you can follow and as soon as you set foot into this world, you will begin getting bombarded with different ideas, advertisements, and proposals. I've tried my best below to take you through it step by step, to come up with a personalized, methodical approach– my advice for you is to follow this guidance before allowing yourself more room for independent manoeuvre.

Let's first begin by examining what stocks actually are – if you are comfortable with your knowledge on this matter, feel free to skip to the next paragraph. A "stock" is a fraction of a company – a tiny slice of a big cake. When you buy a stock, you buy a little piece of the company. You do this because you either anticipate the company doing well and consequently, the value of your stock going up, or because this company pays out fair dividends to its shareholders. A dividend is a monetary "thank you for holding our stock" reward given out by the company to its shareholders. In some cases, your stock may also give you voting rights – you, as a shareholder, have some right to decide the company's trajectory. For now, though, don't worry too much about voting rights – as a stock market beginner, this won't be in your immediate field of interest. The above will do for now as a brief summary – let's move onto the specifics.

Various Strategies and the Three Questions.

The stock market is so big and universal, that the "three questions" mentioned in Chapter 3 apply not only when choosing it as one of your asset types, but when choosing instruments within the stock market too. Note how I use the "three questions" in outlining the strategies below and begin asking them yourselves.

Remember our first question – "How soon do I want a return on my money?" Well, it's time to ask yourself this, and be reasonable about it. Everyone would like a million dollars and preferably tomorrow, or even later today. Unfortunately, this isn't how things work. You need to make a valued judgement about how soon you're looking for a return from the stock market, bearing in mind your specific life circumstances. I would suggest that for most readers, my "Midterm Investing" strategy is most appropriate, but to encapsulate more of my audience, I will outline two other options.

The "Want Cash Today" Approach – Day Trader Strategy.

Quite a few people message me on Instagram for advicw on how to trade and many are surprised to learn that I am not a trader. Then telling them they probably shouldn't be trading either, throws them off completely: isn't day trading **the** way to make big & quick cash? Spoiler: you will not be getting cash *today*. In fact, many days (probably even months) will pass before you will start making same-day-cash. In my eyes, day-trading is the hardest, most time consuming, most math-intense pathway out there. Nonetheless, it's very suitable for some people, and if you are willing to spend generously on training courses and books and are prepared to lose quite a bit of money as part of your learning curve, you should go ahead. The intent of this book is to provide decision-guiding intelligence, not a "Day Trading 101" and as such, I won't be *teaching* you day trading – I have insufficient expertise and experience to do so on a professional level. I will, however, lay out some fundamental aspects of this craft to help you make an informed decision about whether this strategy is right for you.

There are three things you need to become a day trader: some time, a computer and a brain. Time will often be the first hurdle which most do not cross. You first need a lot of time to become knowledgeable enough to day trade – I mean hundreds of hours of reading, learning and practicing. You then need, unsurprisingly, a free day – and not just one, but many free days, during which you can trade in market hours (which is usually about 8 hours). Even if you don't trade for the entire period of open market, you'd still want to be available during the meaty parts of the trading day such as at opening, closing and peak volume trading times. Day trading is, in my eyes, incompatible with university or a full-time job. Having a computer is pretty self-explanatory, so let's talk about the brain. While everyone reading this technically has one, few will find success in employing it as a day trader. The reason why I listed the brain last (in order of importance) is because none of the skills required for day trading are ones demanding natural talent – almost all of them are developed through brute-force learning and experience. As such, you will need to have sufficient understanding of mathematics and be comfortable with charts. Loads of charts. Even then, the odds are against you. Less than four percent of day traders succeed in making day trading their source of living. Most of my friends who tried day trading are now doing something else. But then again, I do know a very small number of people who achieve 20% monthly returns on their capital and are driving Aston Martins.

When you're a day trader, you essentially don't care about the fundamentals of the company. You don't care about the business that the company is doing, you don't care about the industry, you don't care about their management. All you care about is what the market forces are doing to some or other security today. You get used to drawing and analysing charts like these:

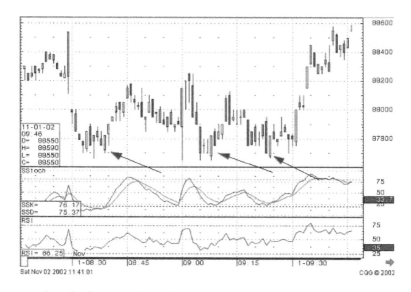

Looks a little complicated, doesn't it? You also have to draw trend channels, resistance, and support lines and much, much more. You have to interpret indicators such as the Relative Strength Index (RSI above) and predict market moves. In short, it's a lot of work and there are quite a few things to remember. But if, having read the above, this sounds like something you fancy, then by all means go ahead. It's certainly better than doing nothing! Though my personal experience in this field is less extensive than that in others, to those of you who do proceed with day trading, I highly recommend the MACD indicator – every single time I got to use it (which is not too often) it has not failed me.

I have limited knowledge about specific & technical risks involved in day trading – the biggest risk is starting day trading in the first place. We have, nonetheless, answered two of the "three questions" with respect to day trading: we defined the time frame and have come to an understanding that here, you *will have to spend lot of time working* for your money. Remember, your chances of success in day trading are very slim. To the vast majority of my readers, far more sustainable and realistic approaches described further in this chapter are more suitable. But if you want to try, best of luck. It's certainly not impossible for you to excel.

The "Midterm Investing" Approach – For Most of Us

My own definition of "midterm" is anything between six months to three years. This approach, I would think, should be the most popular amongst my readers. It appeals to people primarily by low time commitment costs – once you have a grasp of the basics, it only takes you a few days to research a company and make a decision. Then you wait and monitor your investment (which only takes a few minutes and can be done 2-3 times a week) by reading up on relevant news and checking stock price movements. Then, if all is well, you pocket a 10-20% gain a few months or years down the line. You get a tangible gain within a tangible time frame.

To reinstate the "three questions" methodically: this investment strategy provides a return on your capital within a (roughly) three-year time period and requires substantially less daily commitment (that *hard* work) than day trading.

With midterm investing, the third "Risk Question" becomes much more relevant, *technically*. If you chose this strategy, it really should be one of the key factors driving your decision-making. In essence, the question you should ask yourself is this: "What percent of invested capital can I handle losing?" By "handle" I don't mean "get over being sad" about it. I mean, if you lose this money, are you going to have to skip meals or noticeably decrease your standards of living to be able to invest again? If the answer is yes, I want you to re-think how you are reading this book. You know by now that your most important asset is your mind and its ability to function effectively is dependent upon a healthy and consistent lifestyle. Never take on more risk than you can handle – you will not end up in a good place.

Remember, as with any investment, you should always be *hypothetically* prepared for losing everything on the stock market. But be *practical* in objectively assessing your risk tolerance. I would suggest the adequate range of "Capital I'm willing to lose" should be between 20 and 60 percent. From personal experience: if you're not willing to *lose* 20% of your portfolio, you similarly won't be *making* 20% annual returns. Risk, as unnerving as it gets, does pay, so you need to incorporate it into your strategy in a controlled way.

Of course, risk tolerance will vary massively amongst my readers and to help you identify yours, I will employ two extreme 'real-life' examples.

Let's say I have a friend named Brocco who is a 19-year-old university student in the United Kingdom. Brocco's family is really quite wealthy, and he is very far from financial hardship. He receives pocket money charitably from his parents and has 20,000 dollars sitting on his platinum Amex card.

Usually, Brocco would spend his money on clubbing, weekend getaways and shopping sprees, but having read "The Capitalist Manifesto," he decides to go ahead with the "Midterm Investment" strategy with 20,000 dollars. I would estimate Brocco's risk tolerance to be very high – 60 to 70 percent, perhaps even 90. The reasoning is quite simple: if all comes to worst, all that can happen is Brocco walking around with a frowny face for a few days (and maybe sitting through an inconsequential telling-off by his parents). Then he gets more pocket money and, perhaps, a nice lump sum for Christmas – and that's his financial and mental recovery done. Brocco can afford to lose this money and consequently, he can afford to invest into high-risk stocks. If he has been diligent in conducting his research, or even simply got lucky, his returns would be tremendous. His higher-than-average risk tolerance will often translate into higher-than-average profit if he does his homework.

Picture another portrait: a lovely girl called Lilian. She is 22 years old and is currently on full-time employment in Boots Pharmacy. Lilian is the kindest soul on earth, but she was never blessed with rich parents. Having followed "Manifesto's" advice of reducing expenses by 10% and saving up for investment, she managed to aggregate a sum of 1000 pounds after eight months. This is a lot of money to her – to collect another thousand, she'd have to limit her spending for another 8 months. Consequently, her risk tolerance is lower – I would say, between 20 and 25 percent. This means she can only afford to lose a quarter of her portfolio, while the rest of it should be put into safer, less volatile, securities.

The reality is, you – the reader, are probably somewhere in between Brocco and Lilian. Use common sense to assess your situation and estimate your own risk tolerance. We now proceed to examine two examples of companies listed on the New York Stock Exchange with different risk levels – and, consequently, different investment opportunities available to my dear friends.

Our first company is Nio Corporation – a Chinese electric vehicle (EV) manufacturer positioning itself as Tesla's competitor. Having done some basic background research on the EV industry in China, and Nio's position in the market, we can conclude this is a high-risk company – there are plenty of EV manufacturers present and thus, the company faces fierce competition. It also concedes to Tesla in terms of its brand and a reduction in Chinese government support for EVs makes Nio's future is ambiguous. Take a look at the stock chart below – price movements reflect the uncertainty surrounding the company.

As you can see above, Nio's debut on the stock markets was characterized by aggressive gains as the stock price doubled from $6 to $12 – such rapid and dynamic price movements could even be capitalized on by day traders (perhaps justifying the craft for some of you willing to make a short but risky play). This is explained by initial investor optimism about Nio's prospects, specifically, its ability to pose competition to Tesla in China and the expected launch of their new SUV vehicle. The stock then took a nosedive as investor confidence dissipated, followed by a less volatile rebound marked by the second set of arrows. The third set of arrows shows another dramatic upward swing in the stock price, which was later pushed back down to make lower lows by negative press coverage. In summary, there is very significant fluctuation in the stock price (as much as 50/60%) within a relatively short time period (less than one year).

This makes Nio's stock *volatile* – substantial changes in share price make it a risky investment. A good metric to assess the volatility of any particular stock is its beta value (beta is a measure of a stock's volatility in relation to the market). By definition, the market has a beta of 1.0 and stocks are measured in relation thereof; the higher the beta value, the higher the risk. Nio's beta value currently stands at 3.94, meaning the stock is, on average, almost 4 times more volatile than the broader market.

his company could do very well for Brocco. Undoubtedly, buying Nio stock would be a dangerous and speculative move, but providing we know Brocco's situation, we assume he can afford to make this bet. Furthermore, if he is diligent in conducting his research about the company and spends several hours analysing available data (such as earnings estimates, analyst recommendations, quarterly reports, competitors etc.), he can mitigate his risk exposure. The more he knows about the investment he is trying to make, the less likely he is to make a mistake.

Goldman Sachs – one of the most respected and globally ac-claimed investment banks – is bullish (optimistic) on Nio and sets a target price of 13$ per share by 2020. If Brocco invests 70% of his portfolio (14,000$) into Nio stock right now, when it's trading at its all-time lows (3$) and Goldman Sachs' estimates come true, his stake will quadruple in value to 60,000$ within just a few months. His prof-it will amount to roughly 45,000$ which is great news for Brocco (and perhaps his parents who, temporarily, might enjoy a reduction of his strenuous pocket money demands).

On the other hand, a converse scenario is quite possible whereby the share price slides further, making Nio a penny stock company (when the shares are trading at less than $1). In this misfortunate circumstance, Brocco's 14,000$ will turn into 4,500$, or maybe even less. As sorrowful as this may be, we – bearing in mind Brocco's high-risk tolerance – will shrug our shoulders and say, "Those are the rules of the game, buddy..." I want to emphasize my very simple thesis: if your risk tolerance is high, take advantage of it and make risky investments. High risk – high reward.

Having given Brocco plenty of our time, we should check back in on our dear Lilian. She doesn't have high-risk tolerance – does that mean she's not allowed to buy Nio stock and has to miss out on this explosive growth opportunity? Well, not exactly. While she shouldn't put 70% of her hard-earned £1000 into such a high-risk instrument, she can still cash in on potential growth. If she decides her risk tolerance to be at 20%, putting £200 into Nio will still deliver her a juicy percentage gain the same as Brocco's. Of course, the absolute value of her profit will only be £600 which is minute compared to Brocco's $45,000, but remember: she started with much less and allocated Nio a smaller fraction of her portfolio. I'm sure she'd be delighted with her 600 pounds and would orderly reinvest her profits.

But what about the other 80% of Lilian's portfolio? What sorts of lower-risk investment should she be looking for? This is where our second NYSE example comes in and our company is one all of you know: Apple Inc.

Apple is very different to Nio in several ways. Apple is gigantic. It is an established company with history dating back to 1976. It is the world's second-largest smartphone company, world's largest technology company by revenue and one of the world's most valuable companies. Apple, unlike Nio, has a strong position in the market which it more or less sustains. It also differs from Nio in its profitability – Apple's gross profits increased year-on-year for the past four years. Take a look at the 3-year stock price chart:

Apple's strong market position, increasing profits and product diversification (iPhone sales now only constitute 48% of Apple's revenue as opposed to previous highs of almost 70%) are reflected in the upward trend in its stock price. Shown by the green lines is the general trend movement – the last three years have been very positive for Apple. Unlike NIO, Apple is a less risky investment – disregarding the December 18 sell-off (which had little to do with Apple specifically and is mainly explained by the whole stock market turning very sour for a brief time period) – the stock price generally maintains a relatively stable vector. My thesis here is backed by Apple's beta value of 1.08, signifying that its stock is only marginally more volatile than the rest of the market.

An even "safer" company than Apple with respect to beta values would be a company like Tyson Foods: its beta is only at 0.43, making it almost half as volatile as the market. I'll cover more of the beta metric alongside other indicators in the next chapter, but hopefully, by reading through the above comparisons, you've gotten some idea about how beta values can be used to assess risk level of a stock.

Just before we move onto why Apple could be a better choice for Lilian, I want to briefly address the 2018 November – December price dip shown in the chart above. It raises an important theme related to risk management – a bearish stock market and its implications for investors.

In Chapter 2, when I talk about being *specifically knowledgeable* about your investments, I mention that when you own a stock in a company like Apple, not only are you a stakeholder in that company, you are also a stakeholder in the US stock market and the broader economy. This explains the November stock price dive we see above – the hit taken by all stakeholders of the US markets (caused by investor fears fuelled by some technical & political concerns) translates into your personal hit as the stakeholder of the company. Apple is the "A" of the FANG stocks – a group of massive industry-leading technology companies also comprised from Facebook, Netflix and Google. FANG stocks often take a hard blow when the stock market turns bearish (pessimistic). All this is important because it links back to our risk question and asset choices – as investors, Lilian, Brocco, me, and you should be prepared for value fluctuations which are beyond our control and have little to do with the decisions we made. The key here is to remain calm and cold-headed: investment choices made on emotional basis usually turn out to be unsuccessful. If the whole market is plummeting, there's nothing you can do, it will rebound sooner or later; but selling a good company at a loss out of fear would be a mistake.

Many analysts, bankers, and investors (including myself) antic-ipate a strong pullback in US stock markets within one or two years and potentially a recession. Therefore, it may well be the case that Apple's stock will once more plummet forcefully, and it may even break the green-line trend drawn in the chart above. Remember though, this doesn't take away from our fundamental outlook on Apple's business. As mid-term investors, we should be prepared for bearish markets and accept the fact that they may delay our returns.

Now, let's address why Apple's stock is more suited to Lilian's portfolio. We've already discussed how Apple's position differs to that of Nio with respect to its profitability, competitive market share, and establishment level. While this does mean Apple's stock price is un-likely to triple within a few months (which is a very possible scenario for Nio) due to limited "explosive" growth potential, it also means that it probably won't halve (which is also probable for Nio). The most likely trajectory for Apple within our "midterm" time frame would be continuation of its positive upward trend, possibly with fluctuations within the pre-set channel. This makes Apple's stock a great investment for Lilian – mitigated risk and optimistic outlook for the near future could easily reward her with a 10-20% gain. The fact that Apple is such a big and well-known company means it's also more widely covered by banks and analysts - this gives Lilian more data to consider and consequently come up with a more informed conclusion about whether she is poised for pleasant returns shall she decide to buy into Apple stock.

The "Long-term Investing" Approach

We should start off by acknowledging that "Long" and "Midterm" investing strategies are not mutually exclusive – moreover, they often complement each other nicely. While they differ greatly in terms of their time frames (2-3 years vs 10-20 years), the fundamental research you have to conduct for your companies isn't too dissimilar. There are some factors that, unlike with midterm investing, you should omit when considering candidates for long term investments, but ultimately, you're still looking for a good business with high growth potential. For example, our anticipation of a recession outlined previously could deter us from making a *midterm* investment because the stock of a company we're buying is likely to be worth less within this given time frame. On the other hand, we shouldn't care too much about recession risks if we're investing for the *long term*. I personally have several long-term positions comprised of companies I place great trust into, and I have little doubt they'll yield me fantastic returns (despite the fact that I see myself mostly as a midterm investor). Consider combining the two strategies.

Long-term investing, in my eyes, is the least risky since it's less affected by broader market crashes and unreasonable investor sentiment. In essence, if you find and invest into a great business at an early-enough stage of its development, you *will make money*. Just to give you an idea: if you had invested $100 in Amazon right after its IPO in 1997, when its shares were trading at just $18 per share, your stake (taking into account stock splits) would be worth roughly $120,800 in August 2018, yielding you a 120,000% return. Impressive, right?

What a sweet and easy cash machine! Low risk, high return! Why isn't everyone doing this then?

Well, there is a big catch: nobody wants to get rich slow. Nobody wants to wait for twenty years for their investment to bring results, even if they are as gigantic as hundreds of thousands of percent in returns. Warren Buffet is a prime example of how long-term investments can generate exceptional fortunes. For years, Buffet was just an intelligent financier with a net worth of several million dollars. Nothing *too* special. Except for the fact that Warren was, mundanely yet persistently, pumping money into companies like Gillette, Coca-Cola, and later Amazon and Apple. Then, his fortune grew exponentially. His net worth is now at a sexy $81 billion and Berkshire Hathaway (Warren's conglomerate company) is trading at $300,000 per share. Warren Buffet is living proof that "boring" long-term investments can make you very, very rich.

Then there's another catch: Amazon was just one of the 654 companies which IPO'd in 1997. While it has been an exceptional success, it's rise to stardom has quite literally been *except*ional in its nature; meaning, most companies that IPO'd in 97 did okay, some did very well, some failed, but no company performed like Amazon. This is why it may be a little unfair to tease you with the "120,000% return" statistic above – it makes it seem as though you only needed patience and $100 to enjoy profits of $120,000 twenty years down the line. In reality, you needed to have chosen Amazon as *the* company to make a bet on – and that's the harder part. The key was, amid overhype & overvaluation of internet firms, to find a company with a feasible business model, adequate management and good culture. Jeff Bezos – the CEO and founder of Amazon – unlike most entrepreneurs and investors getting caught up in the dotcom mania, selected a narrow niche market: books. Bezos was going to use the internet to sell books, and he was going to become the best at it; simple and plain. But as it turned out, better than pitching complex "internet" business models which promised to transform the global economy but in reality, lacked substance and clear vision. Once Bezos effectively monopolized the online book market, he moved onto peripheral products like office supplies, magazines, and stationery. As such, step by step, Bezos built the world's biggest online retail store which today sells practically everything (including data through Amazon Web Services). The lesson here is: generally, the simpler a start-up's concept is, the clearer its way of making money, the better. Making big promises to investors at an early stage inevitably means either living up to them or failing, and most do the latter.

But even if you didn't bet on Amazon, it's not the end of the world. Amazon was a unique investment opportunity and thus, by definition, not everyone got their hands to it. Even Warren Buffet – the "Oracle of Omaha" – missed out initially, citing his conservative investment ideology as validation for passing on the internet "gamble." But long-term investing can deliver spectacular returns even if you don't spot a gemstone akin to Amazon, and it's not that hard either – it's actually just common sense (and maybe a pinch of intuition). For instance, when Buffet was investing into Gillette in 1989, his assessment metrics were relatively simple. It was easy for him to imagine what the business would look like in 10 years: regardless of what happened to the internet, people would still need to shave. Gillette's strong market share and good management gave Buffet exactly what he was looking for: in his eyes, Gillette would be able to sustain its supernormal profits which it would then use to expand its product range and operation sites, which would then cause more supernormal profits ultimately resulting in company growth. So, Buffet bought $600 million worth of Gillette's stock and bagged a gain of $4.4 billion (excluding dividends) by 2005. The moral of the story is really quite basic: find a good business, wait for ten or fifteen years, get great returns.

Nowadays, most analysts wouldn't even consider Gillette a high growth potential enterprise since it isn't a technology company. In my view, high growth potential companies are mostly tech – the kind like Amazon. Gillette had a good business, but it did nothing revolutionary. Amazon, on the other hand, turned the world of retail upside down. Nonetheless, as exemplified by Buffet's pleasing gain, even companies which don't exactly do anything too spectacular can make you rich if you are willing to *wait long enough.*

Dividend-Seeking Investments:

I dedicate a separate section to dividend investments because they are not bound by time frames. With exception of day trading, dividend investments can complement any combination of mid and long-term exposure one has in their portfolio. I would assume most people know what dividends are, but here's a brief reminder (just in case): a dividend is a monetary pay-out made by a company to its shareholders using the company's profits or cash reserves. Dividends are typically paid as a reward for shareholders' trust or as an unofficial stimulus to boost the stock price.

Not all companies pay them – take Google as the first example that comes to mind: it is sitting on $100 billion in cash and has made $30 billion in profit in 2018, and yet, despite this, despite mounting pressures from shareholders and despite the norms imposed by industry standards, it has to this day restrained from dividend pay-outs. Some companies that do pay dividends may pay them only to certain shareholders: if there is a split between preferred shares (which tend to be more expensive and grant guaranteed dividend priority) and ordinary shares (or A vs B shares), a company may choose to reward the preferred stock owners only. Lastly, a company can also impose a dividend reinvestment plan whereby the pay-outs you are supposed to receive are converted into more company stock, thereby increasing your stake.

So, why do you need dividend stocks in your portfolio? Let's do some simple math: assume you bought 100 shares in AT&T (a US telecom conglomerate) on September 1st, 2018. Your purchase price per share was $31.94 and the total value of your AT&T position was $3,194. Now the stock is trading at $37.79 and so in just over a year, you've bagged a nice gain of 18.3% ($585) gain, as the total value of your stock is now $3,779. That's nice! But in the broad scheme of things, companies like AT&T aren't attractive because of stock price growth. What's more important here is that while holding their stock, you would have also received $254 in dividend income – $50 for every quarter. In total, therefore, your 15-month gain would add to $840 which is more than a quarter of your initial 3.2k investment. Decent, right?

What you do with that income is entirely up to your discretion. Some of you may use the quarterly pay-outs to treat yourselves for being good money masters. Though this isn't the smartest decision you can make, it sometimes is necessary – the fact that you have real money pouring into your account every three months is both gratifying and tempting. We will talk more about what to do with gains in the "Spending Habits" chapter; but don't forget: dividends are your "children." Instead of "killing" them all on thrilling lattes and scallop sushi rolls, try putting (most of) them back into your "money factory" and make them give you grandkids.

For instance, you could use dividend income to increase your risk tolerance – you know by now that higher risk comes with higher reward – so maybe make a play on a risky stock or even a cryptocurrency. What if you win? What if, as a result of your *informed gamble*, those $200 you invested into bitcoin double in value? More children and grandchildren! You've used your pay-out income to take a risk which you wouldn't otherwise carry – see how your opportunities expand thanks to dividends?

There are several high-yield companies out there. Not to complicate things; you can find them by googling "best dividend stocks" and browsing around. I've given you what you need to know about dividends – they can most certainly be a precious addition to your portfolio.

Stock Analysis "Cheat Sheet"

To help with your analysis of different companies, I have created an oversimplified yet (hopefully) useful table of the most fundamental measures you should fill out each time when considering buying a stock. Metrics like "Industry" and "Earnings Growth" should give you insights about growth potential, "Dividends" (or lack thereof) will remind you of the nature of your investment (such as dividend-seeking or growth-seeking), while "Investment Horizon" and

"Beta Value" answer to the time frame and risk aspects of our "three questions."

Bear in mind, I will list all platforms that can and should be used for obtaining the information to fill these tables in the Epilogue.

There are two tables; one I have filled in myself for you to use as an example, the other is to be filled in by you when needed. Below, I have compared two companies from the same industry with *very* different outlooks for the near future. Take a look:

STOCK NAME:	Kellogg International	Kraft Heinz
STOCK TICKER & PLATFORM:	NYSE: K	NASDAQ: KHC
INDUSTRY:	Packaged Foods & Meats	Packaged Foods & Meats
INVESTMENT 'HORIZON':	2-3 Years	2-3 Years
OPTIMAL OBJECTIVE RETURN*:	15%	-10%
1-YR PERFORMANCE:	17%	-36%
DIVIDEND & YIELD:	2.28, 3.31%	1.60, 5.2%
ANALYST RECOMMENDATIONS:	2.7 (Weak Buy)	3.7 (Weak Sell)
BETA (RISK) VALUE:	0.55	1.03
EARNINGS GROWTH (YoY or Quarterly):	2% - last 4 beat analyst estimates	-4.8% decline

STOCK NAME:		
STOCK TICKER & PLATFORM:		
INDUSTRY:		
INVESTMENT 'HORIZON':		
OPTIMAL OBJECTIVE RETURN*:		
YTD PERFORMANCE:		
DIVIDEND & YIELD:		
ANALYST RECOMMENDATIONS:		

BETA (RISK) VALUE:		
EARNINGS GROWTH (YoY or Quarterly):		

*Optimal Objective Return is my own metric and essentially answers the question: "How much gain, realistically, are you anticipating to bag?" This figure should be informed by previous price movements (for example, if a stock has only increased 10% over the last year while maintaining strong earnings and its positive trend, it would be unreasonable to set *OOR at 50%) and company dynamics.

Bonds & Debt Instruments:

If the stock market is the "elephant," the debt market is the "whale." Our "whale" receives tangibly less press coverage than our "elephant," yet it is still the biggest mammal on the face of earth. We are now moving onto our second basic security – bonds and other debt instruments. A bond is a fixed-income tradeable security that symbolizes a loan made by the lender to the borrower. It is a contract being traded on the open market that contains details of the loan (such as the date when the principal amount has to be repaid and the fixed or variable interest rates determined by the lender).

For those who want things simpler: Jack borrows $100 from Jill at an interest rate of 3% per annum over a time period of five years. As each year passes, Jack pays Jill $3 (3% x $100) and when the five years are up, he also pays back the principal of $100. If Jack is known to have a poor credit score and an awful track record of timely repayment, Jill will charge him a higher interest rate to compensate for the additional risk she is exposed to. Similarly, if Jack wants to borrow the money for 15 years instead of 5, Jill will again demand higher interest since the opportunity cost of lending that money for longer is greater.

This is the debt market at its core! Now, replace Jack with corporations, municipalities, and sovereign governments (who issue bonds to finance their affairs) and replace Jill with investors (who lend the money to the above in seeking a return).

A quick summary of important definitions:

-   The principal value (also called the face value) of the bond is the amount of money borrowed by an entity (Jack's $100).

-   The coupon value is the annual interest rate paid by the borrower (Jill's condition of 3% per annum).

-   The coupon dates are when annual payments are to be made by the borrower (the date of each year when Jack pays Jill $3).

-   The issue price is the price at which the borrower initially sells the bonds.

-   The maturity date is when the borrower repays the lender the face value of the bond (when Jack pays $100 after 5 years).

-   Yield to Maturity (YTM) is the total return anticipated if the bond is held to its maturity date.

Thus far, we have assumed that Jill will hold the bond for the entire five-year period right up until the maturity date and so the total amount of money she would receive back at the end will add up to $115. But what if Jill needs money right now? What if an emergency happened, or what if she found a great investment opportunity and needs the capital? She returns to the market.

Prices for bonds change every day and fundamentally are affected by varying levels of supply and demand. An increased likelihood of default can cause a reduction in demand for bonds, resulting in lower prices – the inverse also holds true. An increase in government-set interest rates can cause a reduction in demand for bonds, again, leading to lower prices and vice versa.

The global bond market is worth north of 100 trillion dollars (that's actually more than the global stock market) and there is a lot to unpack here – I could ramble on about convertible bonds, zero-coupon bonds, option bonds, debt ETFs and much, much more. Above, I've tried my best to be concise while covering bond basics required for understanding of what's to come in this chapter, namely: how should *you* involve bonds in your investments. I would strongly advise browsing the web to better your understanding of debt instruments and make yourself a more informed bond investor.

Now then, why are bonds good for you? Should you even bother, or will your participation in the stock market suffice? Well, first of all you have to know that oftentimes, the stock and bond markets behave in inverse ways – when equity markets do well, bond markets tend to do badly and vice versa. Therefore, by exposing yourself to both stock *and* debt securities, you mitigate your risk as an investor and somewhat protect your capital in the case of a stock market crash. Secondly, bonds as an asset class are widely regarded to be far less dangerous than stocks. If a company files for bankruptcy, it will prioritize repayment of its creditors (bondholders) over-compensation for its shareholders. Furthermore, if we are talking about government bonds (especially that of the western nations), we should acknowledge these are basically considered foolproof instruments for store of value. There probability of the United States government defaulting on its $23 trillion debt in the foreseeable future (10 years) is virtually zero and so their bonds (with their 2% yields) are seen as very secure instruments. Thirdly, bonds (especially if you intend to hold them until their maturity date) are generally easier to research and buy. Lastly, unlike many stocks, bonds provide you with a regular yearly cash flow – real money you can spend immediately without altering the composition of your portfolio. In essence, it comes down to risk spreading, ease of holding management and the desired extent of cash flow generated by your portfolio on an annual basis. Come to think of it, all of this traces back to my "three Questions" outlined in Chapter 3!

So, search online for bonds you might fancy. Remember to keep in mind the important factors: you want a relatively high bond yield with a relatively low default probability (refer to bond rating agencies like Moody's). Guide your selection by the desired time frame (it can be as little as a few months or as long as 30 years) and the desired risk level. Consider whether your investor profile is more suited to government or corporate bonds. Analyse!

With respect to the proportion of capital allocated to bonds against stocks, we will address that more in my "Sample Portfolio Exercise" section. Just remember, the level of risk you are willing to take is crucial in determining that proportion. You want to play it safe and accept modest returns? 70% bonds – 30% stocks. Want to be a risk monster? 95% stocks – 5% bonds. Figure it out, folks.

Chapter 5:

Non-Basic Securities.

In the previous chapter, we talked about the most widespread & universal securities – stocks and bonds. Quick recap: stocks are units of a company that you can buy in anticipation of the price of that unit increasing (or that company paying out dividends) and bonds are loans with an interest that you make to governments and corporations. I would expect most of my readers to incorporate either one of those (or even better, both!) into your portfolios. This chapter is for those who want to take things up a notch or those with a risk tolerance high enough to dabble with more unconventional instruments.

ETFs

"ETF" stands for Exchange Traded Fund. I could tell you quite a bit about ETFs, but this chapter will be chunky as it is: I'm going to cut straight to the chase and keep things as simple as possible. You should think of ETFs as theme-based "goody bags" tailored for your own purposes by large investment groups like Vanguard and BlackRock. ETFs can consist of virtually anything: oil stocks, government or corporate bonds, emerging markets, index funds (like the S&P500) amongst many other things.

Let's say you want to build your exposure to Robotics and AI. You can either spend hours upon hours searching for companies and hand-picking stocks that suit your needs or you can buy an ETF that has done the hard work for you. A while ago, I did just that and acquired a large position in ARKK innovation ETF (look it up!) – I've made 55% profit without having to worry about what proportion of my funds should be allocated to each type of innovation-based asset because the fund managers handle that for me.

There are high yield ETFs and low yield ETFs. There are expensive ETFs and cheap ETFs. There are also inverse ETFs such as SQQQ (again, Google!) that investors, like myself, can use to be *against* the stock market. The point is that you really can find an ETF for just about any theme, any time frame and any investor profile. It is important you familiarize yourself with this tool, keeping in mind the important metrics used to compare ETFs (such as year-to-date performance, expense ratio, number, and composition of holdings and dividends). Especially for those who are just getting started in the world of investments, ETF's can be easy and convenient like no other. I strongly recommend searching the web for any you might fancy buying!

Derivatives

A derivative is a tradeable security, the price of which is derived from an underlying asset. That asset can be virtually anything – stocks, bonds, currencies, commodities, you name it – and there are thousands of variations of derivatives trading in the open markets. If you want to set yourself a little challenge, try researching and *understanding* swaps and futures contracts – I will not cover these here. What I will cover though are option contracts, which I would assume should be most popular and bring the most utility to my readers. An option contract is an asymmetrical tradeable agreement between two parties, whereas one party has the obligation to buy or sell the underlying asset at a pre-determined price at a later date, whereby the other party can make a choice. There are two types of option contracts – call options and put options. A call option gives you the right (but not the obligation) to buy something at a later date at a given price whereas a put option gives you the right (but not the obligation) to sell something at a later date at a pre-set price. If, instead of buying puts and calls, you sell puts and calls, you will end up on the receiving side of the contract and then you **will** have the obligation to either buy or sell the underlying asset shall your counterparty decide to exercise their option.

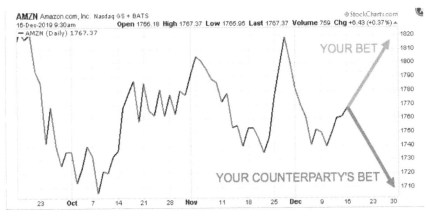

If you are not yet confused, you are probably amongst the few. For those that are, a real-life example should help: let's assume that you are bullish (optimistic) on Amazon and anticipate the stock price to reach $1820 in the near future. The market finds you a counterparty that bets just the opposite – they are bearish (pessimistic)

and think the price will fall to $1710. Take a look at the three-month chart below:

Say you buy a call option (which typically costs a miniscule fraction of the price of the underlying asset) with the expiry date of December 30th and the predetermined price of $1740. When the day comes, you have the right (but not the obligation) to buy X amount of Amazon stock at $1740 per share.

Now, assuming your bet was correct and the price on December 30th is indeed hovering around $1820, then things work out very well for you! You exercise your option and buy the stock from your counterparty (who is obliged to sell it to you) at $1740 per share. You then sell the stock on the open market for its current price of $1820, thereby making a profit of $80 per share sold. Happy days! If, however, your bet proves to be incorrect and Amazon's shares head south, you simply shouldn't exercise your option. In this case, you will incur a small loss of the premium you paid to enter this contract in the first place – nothing too tragic.

We have just covered how purchasing call options allows you to bet on a future price increase without hefty capital commitment. A similar scheme can be used with buying put options when trying to bet *against* an asset – in this case, you would just switch and be the bearish counterparty. Buying protective puts can also be used to protect unrealized gains when investors are still bullish on the stock in the long run, but uncertain of price fluctuations in the nearest future. Let's also quickly address what would change if you were to *sell* call and put options - how can you use that to your advantage?

If you were to sell a call option, you would be selling *an obligation to sell* an asset at a pre-determined strike price at a future date.

You, as the call option writer, would be paid a premium for entering this contract with your counterparty. The idea here is this: you hope that the agreed strike price of the underlying asset is never reached and thereby the option cannot be exercised. This then allows you to simply pocket the premium you have been paid and live happily ever after!

Selling a put option is different – you are still paid a premium for entering the contract, just as above, but this time you are selling *an obligation to buy*. Quite often, I myself sell put options when I find stocks. I'm very optimistic about in the long run and ones which I wouldn't mind holding for several years. Sometimes, my put options are exercised, and I end up having to buy the shares (I'm happy with that anyways), but more often I just bag the premiums and relax.

Derivatives are probably the most technical, most complex concept outlined in both of my "Securities" chapters, so if you managed to get through all this – give yourself a big pat on the back. Even if you didn't quite catch some (or all) of that outlined above, please do not worry! These things take time to understand and digest. Hopefully, I've done a good enough job at explaining for you to have a broad idea of what these instruments can allow you to do. If you feel as though these are tools that you would want to be using regularly, by all means dive into some further reading.

Forex

You've probably heard the word "forex" before and most likely know it stands for "Foreign Exchange." I actually considered talking about forex in my "day-trading" paragraph of the previous chapter because most activity on this market is classed as "trades" as opposed to investments. In a nutshell, what you need to know is this: there are different currencies around the world (US Dollar, Japanese Yen, British Pound, and so on) which trade in pairs with other different currencies (Canadian Dollar, Chinese Yuan, Russian Ruble, etc.). Different geopolitical and economic events cause trading fluctuations of those pairs through an appreciation of one currency or a depreciation of another. For instance, when Russia claimed Crimea (debated Ukrainian territory) in 2014, it was punished by crippling international economic sanctions. The Russian Ruble has since then halved in value against the US dollar – if you were able to predict this devaluation (which shouldn't have been hard at all), you could have profited by betting against the Ruble.

Frankly, forex isn't something I would expect most of my readers to be involved in. There are so many ever-changing variables that have to be taken into account when speculating with currency pairs, it is almost impossible for amateurs to compute. Furthermore, unlike with equities and bonds, you can't exactly enter a long-term position in forex, and if you revisit the last chapter, you will recall that the greatest profit is created by holding value-generating assets for long periods of time. Nonetheless, forex is far too big not to be mentioned – I've done my duty – and to be fair, my disaffection the space is not as strong as that to trading. You can typically hold forex positions for longer (on average) and, if you keep things simple and construct your bets on universal, large-scale geopolitical events (like Brexit, which receives all-too-much media coverage) you can bag some nice profits there. With this said, forex still requires substantial time commitment on a regular basis. Do you want to spend a few hours of your day trying to snatch a couple of percent gains here and there? Be my guest! This may work out just fine for some of you.

Cryptocurrency

Whether crypto can even be dubbed a "security" is debatable, but for the purpose of this section we shall call it so. A few words on what cryptocurrency really is: a decentralized, irreversible and vastly anonymous financial system based on blockchain that circumvents the banks and government in facilitating transactions. The first cryptocurrency ever made was Bitcoin (still the largest coin to this day with $100 billion market cap) as a response to the financial crisis of 2007/8. When released in 2010, it traded for about $0.0008 per coin and has since then peaked at $20,000 in 2018 – such gigantic returns have made men billions and generated buzz in the press. I'm sure you're used to hearing this from me, but once again, I recommend doing further research on what cryptocurrency is and what the investment prospects are. I cover cryptocurrency in more detail in the last chapter of the "Manifesto" and provide my own insights about the future of this market.

I would say the unique thing about digital currencies like bitcoin is that the "time frame" part of the "three questions" really is quite flexible. You can buy and hold Bitcoin for a few years (which is essentially what I did) and hope that amid highly volatile swings you can sell your position for a nice profit. Cryptocurrency as an asset class will no longer bring thousands of percent returns but I still think that at this stage, if you get in on one of the dips (buy low) you can easily make a 50% gain or so in the midterm. With respect to altcoins (coins other than bitcoin of which there are thousands),

I would advise to steer clear of most of them unless you really know what you're doing. Overall, I would consider cryptocurrency a worthy (albeit risky) alternative investment for readers willing to go beyond basic securities and speculate on non-conventional assets.

Venture Capital & Private Equity

Something I've been passionate about and heavily involved in recently is venture capital (VC). As mentioned before, the world of private equity and early-stage investments is one suitable to a small minority of my readers. Most often, to get a good VC deal you have to have sizeable capital at your disposal as well as access to VC people/funds who will pitch to your investment opportunities. Even if you have both, you will still face the most difficult hurdle: VC is *hard*, and the vast majority of start-ups fail. VC requires intuition, experience, resilience to risk, and uncertainty. But it's also where you get your best returns. Forget 20% annualized gains on trading forex: you're looking at returns within the 5x-1000x range. You're looking at unicorn companies.

When you spot your next "Netflix" or "Airbnb" at its venture stage, your gains can be tremendous (and easily tramp returns from any other asset class). You're capturing the most value at a time when the company is in its early native stages – it doesn't get much better than this.

The problem is: you only get *one* "superstar" company for every *twenty* investments that end up failing. Almost all venture capitalists I spoke to identify a similar pattern: in a portfolio of 20 companies: one or two are "superstars," five or six are doing okay (i.e. do bring *some* return) and the success of the rest is either uncertain or explicitly absent altogether. The reason I'm telling you all this is I want to give my favourite field credit where it is due and perhaps even prompt some readers to consider VC as a career or educational interest! It's fun, it can make great money, and it's much more personal than something like speculating on a publicly-traded stock. But yes, it's also incredibly risky and complex to get into – VC is not something you can pick up overnight.

For those rightfully intrigued or drawn by the space, the best way to get started is to learn. Attend VC-themed conferences, try finding and speaking to acquaintances affiliated with the field, and socialize with start-up founders. Perhaps even, depending on where you currently are in life, seek employment at flagship VC funds like Sequoia or Softbank to gain further experience. It may also be worth working in a small (less than 50 people) fund to get a more comprehensive and personal sense of the Venture Capital Industry. We need more venture capitalists!

Real Estate

Last but not least is real estate – again, something that's probably appropriate to a minority of those reading this (due to high upfront capital commitment) and something that strictly speaking is not even a security (though relevant to this chapter, nonetheless). There are essentially two income-generating things you can do with real estate: flip houses or establish rental properties.

Flipping houses goes a little like this: you find an old home and recognize potential, you buy it, you refurbish and renovate it, you list it on the market, you sell it and make a profit. Sounds pretty simple, right? Yeah, except you need the money to buy it with in the first place (unless you can come up with some sort of convoluted mortgage scheme), you certainly need the money for all the construction and renovation, but most importantly, you need the knowledge and the intuition to buy the right house at the right time. While this is no easy skill to learn, it's very much doable. Though I have never done it myself, I know people who regularly make 2-3x returns flipping houses. If combining your inner artist with your inner entrepreneur is something that sounds appealing, I'd advise reading some books on how to do real estate or finding a mentor.

Establishing rental properties is probably a little simpler than flipping houses. More often than not, it requires less up-front capital and is generally seen to be a less risky way of doing real estate. You can either do short-term lets or long-term lets. I myself have an apartment which we bought a decade ago and I've never actually lived in it because we rent it out. That's long term lets – our tenant has been living there for years and has provided us with a stable annual cash flow. Unlike with reselling houses, we do not care whether property prices in London are climbing or plummeting right now – we have a tenant and that tenant pays us well. With short-term lets, you're looking at something like Airbnb – here's a general idea for you: you find a property in a popular area of your town, you rent it for two years (make sure the contract allows subletting), you take nice pictures and list your property on Airbnb. You then pay for advertisements, aggregate great customer reviews and build the online presence. Of course, you can also list your own property if you wish, or even use the profits made to buy more real estate that you can further list on Airbnb. If you do the work diligently, you can make upwards of two ends on your initial investment (cost of the two years rental plus any minor miscellaneous costs). I have a friend called Michael who rakes in roughly £4 million each year from his multiple Airbnb listings in the city of London – this should give you an idea of how well you can do with short-term rentals in big cities.

SAMPLE PORTFOLIO EXERCISE

TOTAL CAPITAL COMMITED: $10,000	
Risk Tolerance: Medium	
Time Frame: Mid-Term (2yrs)	

BASIC SECURITIES = $6500							
STOCKS = $4000					BONDS = $2500		
HIGH RISK STOCKS = $1000	MID RISK STOCKS = $1500	LOW RISK STOCKS = $500	DIVIDEND STOCK = $500	ETFs = $500	GOV. BONDS = $1250	CORP. BONDS = $500	ETFs = $750
$NIO (NIO CORPORATION) $TSLA (TESLA) $BYND (BEYOND MEAT)	$SHOP (SHOPIFY) $TTD (TRADE DESK) $NVDA (NVIDIA) $AMZN (AMAZON)	$AAPL (APPLE) $	$AT&T (TELECOM)	$ARKK	US TREAS 3YR US TREAS 1YR	BP 1 YR	BP 1 YR

NON-BASIC SECURITIES = $3500			
CRYPTO = $2000		DERIVATIVES = $1000	FX SPECULATION = $500
STANDARD COINS = $1500	STABLE COINS = $500	CALLS = $500 / PUTS = $500	
BTC (BITCOIN) ETH (ETHEREUM) XRP (RIPPLE)	USDT (TETHER)	BABA CALL @ $A KO CALL @ $B TOTAL CALL @ $C / SQ PUT @ $X FEYE PUT @ $Y GOLD PUT @ $Z	

Remember how I said I would not spoon-feed you? Well, this is about as close as we will get to that – not only have I made you a snazzy little exemplary table, I've also listed some great asset names in there. If you're not making notes by now, something really is quite wrong.

Below is a blank copy of the above for you to fill in. You can jiggle things around, determine your own risk tolerance & time frame as well as the type of non-basic securities that will comprise your portfolio. For instance, if your "Total Capital Committed" number reaches seven-figures, you might want to drop in "Real Estate" or "Venture Capital" as one of your asset types. Hopefully, this page gives you the broad idea of my concept: specific application of it is in your sole hands. None of this is formal investment recommendation.

	TOTAL CAPITAL COMMITED: _____
	Risk Tolerance:
	Time Frame:

BASIC SECURITIES = $	
STOCKS = $	BONDS = $

Please don't forget to be a global thinker: use both *specific and generic knowledge* to inform the composition of your portfolios. An important thing to keep in mind (especially at this point in time) is that there are several macro-level factors which influence the value of your assets. You can get caught up in all the nitty-gritty's, analyse ratios, and trends but one tweet from the US president can put all of that work to nothing if you do not account for it. Geopolitics can be an ugly force (especially for amateur investors), but a force to be counted with, nonetheless.

Chapter 6:

Mentality

Most books in the personal finance & self-improvement genre go on about some mysterious sort of "mentality" which is supposedly the key to bewildering success. Apparently, it all starts with mentality, and it all ends with it too. Napoleon Hill's best-seller *"Think and Grow Rich"* - inspired by Andrew Carnegie - has sold over 100 million copies worldwide, and it was all about mentality. In my view, the attention given to "mentality" by many authors and "gurus" is blown out of proportion. You can have a fantastic mindset, but unless you are willing and able to act on your thoughts and ideas, you will get nowhere. Nonetheless, having the right mindset is necessary (though not sufficient) for going places in life.

Mentality is one of those themes featured in personal development books which, across the board, gets very, very repetitive. The best reads I could recommend for this topic are *"Principles"* by Ray Dalio and *"Zero to One"* by Peter Thiel. But even then, these two books (which I consider the best of the best) share a few quite similar ideas. They are worth reading, but for "Manifesto's" sake and purpose, this chapter will provide a *shortened* summary of the key dogmas expressed on mentality in self-achievement books.

1: You Can Do It. But Only if You Believe You Can.

As cringe as this sounds, it really is true, and my personal experiences in life have gone to show that. One episode I remember vividly was as such: my parents, whom I've been pestering to get me a puppy as my birthday gift, were out of ways to say "no." Their reasoning was simple: my mother was allergic to dogs and the pup wouldn't be able to stay inside the house – we'd have to build him a separate little house which was a hassle. Moreover, they thought I would forget my "pet chores" and shift responsibility of looking after the animal to someone else. They came up with a clever way of refusing my pressing urges; I was doing karate at the time at a semi-professional level and their ingenious solution was asking that I win an under-13 karate competition. If I win, I get the dog. If I don't, I have to think of something else to ask for my birthday. There was just one catch: I was a ten-year-old competing with 11 and 12-year-olds. At this age especially, these three to four-year gaps make a tremendous difference. In the eyes of my trainer, that was impossible. In the eyes of my parents, they've figured out a smart way to cut the "dog talk" for good. Odds were stacked against me. But I **really** wanted the dog and I **believed** that I could win. The "it's tough," "probably not," and "when you're older" maybes went into one ear and right out of the other. On the big day, to the shock of my trainer and my parents, I won. There and then, I learnt one of my most treasured lessons: *the "impossible" is only unachievable until you achieve it.* It's just a word. You *can* do anything. This book is about money, but this approach is applicable in each and every aspect of life. You *can* be the greatest at what you do, be it art, science or whatever else. You have to just *want it bad enough.*

Look at Jack Ma. After college, he applied to 30 different jobs and got rejected from every single one. This also includes his application to work in KFC – out of the 24 people that applied, Ma was the only one who didn't get the job. He then applied to Harvard ten times and ten times he got rejected. Ma was, by most measures, a failure - a man kept being punched in the face with life's rough boxing gloves. But Ma believed. He had a vision and a good work ethic. In 1999, Jack Ma and his team of 17 friends started Alibaba.com in his Hangzhou apartment. Today, it's China's biggest online retailer and is valued at $430 billion on the NYSE, while Ma's personal net worth is at $38 billion. A classic "rags to riches" story (one of **many**) – just goes to show that *anyone,* even those rejected by KFC, can make it.

Do not be afraid to know your worth, to exploit your strong sides and to dream big. If you believe in yourself and your dreams, you're off to a good start.

2: The Concept of Rationality

Rationality is a concept I'm personally very fond of, but for some reason, it's rarely covered in its pure form in financial literature. A decision can either be rational or irrational. You can either be robotic and mechanical or emotional and impulsive. Rationality is all about computing the most relevant inputs within a given situation, and then making a decision through a chain of reasoning. To exemplify: buying a Louis Vuitton x Supreme T-Shirt for $1200 is an irrational and impulsive decision because it's primarily driven by your emotional desires: you know you're only paying for the logo on a piece of cotton that cost pennies to make, and yet you choose to spend this amount of money to stroke your ego, feel recognized, or appear wealthy. Another irrational decision could be taking a black cab instead of the tube when travelling to work – you know you'll probably get to your destination in the same time, but because you *perceive* the cab to be more convenient or luxurious, you go with it. A rational, "robotic" decision would be something like this: in searching the web for a new microwave that *you need,* you visit several websites, compare prices and brand quality, look at delivery times, and bearing in mind what you want from this purchase, make an informed choice.

In order to practice rationality, you need to create *prioritized criterion.* Let's say your prioritized criteria is saving more money for your investments. Basing your rational thinking off these criteria, each time you spend, you should ask yourself these questions: "Is this a rational purchase?", "Do I actually need this?", and "Why am I buying this?" Be honest in answering yourself and remember: rationality and emotion-driven thinking are not friends. If the answer to any of these questions conflict with your criterion, a rational decision would take that into account. Sweep aside your personal biases, habits, and inclinations and try thinking like a machine. Compute only the input *strictly* relevant to a specific situation (i.e. do not consider: "will I look cool on Instagram if I post a boomerang of this matcha latte," instead consider: "I only need a coffee to wake up, so I'm not spending $10 on a Starbucks drink"). Make the most rational decision possible. This way, you will get closer to achieving your prioritized criterion.

Rationality applies everywhere, not just purchases. Its implementation makes life easier, more convenient and coherent. It even comes into play in the most mundane situations. Let's say you have to pick your headphones up from a friend that lives two hours away from you – you can either wait for him to come back into town five days from now and borrow a pair from your sister meanwhile, or you can make the trip down to pick them up. While it may be more *comfortable and fun* for you to have a little road trip to see your buddy, grab a drink with him and pick up your headphones, it's far more *rational* for you to use your sisters for the few days and wait for him to come back into the city. You'll save yourself some fuel, a morning hangover and most importantly, time, which could be spent on far more valuable activities. When making decisions guided by rationality (ideally, the vast majority of all decisions you make), try imagining balanced weight scales and put the "cons" and "pros" on either side. The mechanism that tilts the scales is rational thinking: what's more important and more aligned with my prioritized criterion? Be rational!

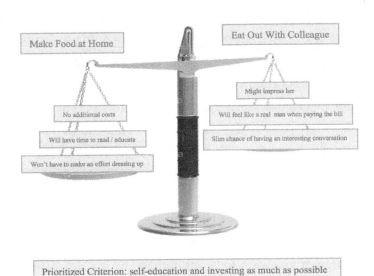

Make Food at Home

Eat Out With Colleague

Might impress her

No additional costs

Will feel like a real man when paying the bill

Will have time to read / educate

Slim chance of having an interesting conversation

Won't have to make an effort dressing up

Prioritized Criterion: self-education and investing as much as possible

3: The Concept of Objectivity

Another concept closely linked with rationality is *objectivity*. Objectivity is all about the way you see things and what you make of them. True objectivity involves extending the principles of rational thinking from just decision-making to interpretation of events and situations. To illustrate my point, I'll ask you to picture the following scenario: the weather forecast predicts heavy rainfall all across the the country in the upcoming week. For a subsistence farmer, this is excellent news – he won't need to be using his precious reservoirs to water the crops because the rain will do it for him. For a newspaper boy working in the city, the forecast is terrible: not only will it be gloomy and wet outside, but his newspapers will also get ruined by the rain and he will get less sales. Both views are *subjective*: they take a neutral event (rain) and classify it as either good or bad based on pre-existing conditions such as emotional response, level of convenience (or lack thereof) caused by the event, and other biases. From an *objective* viewpoint, all that's going to happen is rain. Nothing more; nothing less. You, as an objective thinker, need to realize this and attempt to mute your pre-programmed ideas and emotions when assessing and responding to an event. **For almost all people, what you see depends on who you are.** In being objective, remove the "you" part. *This way, you'll see all events as they really are – **neutral**, and in the broad scheme of things, a lot less significant than you make them out to be in the heat of the moment.* Once you achieve objectivity in your thinking, *you* can make an informed call on whether you want to be a newspaper boy or a farmer (or maybe, even whether you want to be on holiday during the rainy times).

4: Being Open-Minded

The topic of objectivity leads us on nicely to *radical open-minded-ness* – a concept coined by Ray Dalio in *"Principles"* (by now, if the number of times I've mentioned this book hasn't given you any hints: it **really** is worth reading). The name of this concept is pretty self-explanatory: extreme open-mindedness is one of the key habits we all need to develop. Open-mindedness does not mean not having an opinion, nor does it entail avoiding disagreements. Actually, when open-minded people meet face to face, you will quite often see a debate or intellectual contest. While this may appear inherently contradictory, two people can strongly disagree with each other while remaining radically open-minded.

In my interpretation, open-mindedness is more about how broad your scope of view is. Not only do you have an opinion, you can evaluate it too: you can understand and explain why you think a certain way, where this view stems from, why your view may be flawed and to what extent it makes sense to other people. You have to be able to do this with views of others: step into their shoes and see things from their perspective. This will allow you to discover things you haven't seen before.

I have never been a fan of contemporary art. To me, random shapes, crooked sculptures from plastic straws and plain canvases never made much sense and certainly did not classify as art. I just could not see how a sensible human being would pay $60 million for a black square that claimed to be a "masterpiece." I can make a black square! Why is mine not worth that much then? Anyhow, just recently, I've attended an art event which involved some of world's most renowned contemporary artists bringing their work and explaining the journey they went through when creating it. To save you time, I won't outline the chronicles told by the artists and skip will right on to the moral of the story: I've somewhat understood how their work in fact is **art**. Most of the time, there was a powerful message, some sort of back story which preceded each art piece and all of a sudden, objects which just five minutes ago were pieces of garbage in my eyes, began making much more sense. Some were even…. beautiful. I doubt this transformation in my mind goes as far as to justify $60 million valuations, but at least now I'm willing to call contemporary work *art* and mean it.

This only happened because I tried to be open-minded. I suppressed my scepticism and ignored the "freaky" outfits which almost every single contemporary maestro was wearing that evening. I tried to listen and *hear* (the two are not the same), to see things from their angle. It worked!

5: Ego and Blind Spots

There are, however, some things which stand in the way of being *radically open-minded,* and those things are called: *blind spots and ego.* Everyone has an ego. It varies in size and expressiveness among different people, but we all have it, nonetheless. Ego is "I know better." Ego is "I'm smarter than her." Ego is "Look at me, I'm really cool and therefore am right." A lot of us stroke our ego without even realizing it. Have you ever done something nasty– like being mean to someone - and then immediately thought "why the hell did I do this? There was no need for that whatsoever…." That was your ego showing its head, trying to make itself feel more present, tricking you into feeling a certain type of way (such as "down with the cool kids").

To some people (not excluding myself), big ego can be a detriment if not handled properly. If you are too convinced in your excellence, knowledge and superiority, if you are unable to tune in to the world around you, you'll struggle to be open-minded. The first step in taming your ego is recognizing it when it shows. Think about yourself for a minute: would people say you have a big ego? Do you? How much do you love yourself? How confident are you in what you do in your day to day life? How is your ego expressed? If you are someone that has literally been a failure up to this point in their lives and haven't achieved much at all, *tell yourself that*. If your self-esteem is disproportionately high compared to your actual achievements, *tell yourself that*. Be **honest**. Your ego will screech in pain, but you'll also have a very humbling experience. It's hard to discover you are not the best, not unique, not special and frankly pretty mediocre. But it's a necessary discovery and once made, you're on your way to tremendous improvement. The trouble is, most people find these things very difficult to say to themselves because their ego takes the best of them. Try avoiding this trap if you want a change.

Our discussion of ego takes us smoothly onto the second biggest obstacle to open-mindedness: *blind spots*. These "spots" are certain things or perspectives we cannot see, and they stem from our ego and our background. Once again, everyone has blind spots, and on varied levels. By law of nature, some people are good at some things and terrible at others. It would be difficult to explain to a pottery artist why IBM's quantum computer is of such great importance to humankind. The pottery artist is innately inadept to science and its methods. Over the years of struggling with physics in high school and failing to appropriately close accounting books for his pottery shop, he has learned to stay away from science for good. It's very hard to get the potter *excited* about the quantum computer; he has a blind spot and therefore cannot (and does not want to) see the revolutionary nature of this discovery.

Dalio's mention of blind spots focuses more on interpersonal communication rather than crafts of different professions. This makes sense: blind spots (and their incompatibility) are the root cause of breakdowns in relationships of every sorts. They originate from your upbringing, the principles and values instilled (or not) in you by your parents and your past experiences and beliefs. The more I think about them, the more I see them. For example, I am someone that tends to prioritize result over effort. Achievement is important to me. So, when I ask a friend to pick up my wallet from her sister's house and, despite seeing me several times and having lots of fun enjoying each other's company, she continually fails to bring me the wallet, I get annoyed. She gets annoyed too because I "give her a hard time" even though she has tried several times to pick the thing up from her sister's house but was evidently prevented from doing so by some logistical mishap. In her eyes, she is right to be annoyed: I'm being an ungrateful swine since not only have I forgotten the wallet in the first place, I'm also giving her a pounding about something that's not exactly her fault. "My sister wasn't home, but I did go down there... See, I tried!"

Blind spots. She is blind to my perspective and I am blind to hers. To me it's pretty simple: she said she'd get it, it's been two months and I'm still wallet-less. I want result. To her it's simple too: her sister is a separate person with a separate agenda and obtaining the wallet is not solely down to my friend's control. She made several attempts, and to her that is what matters. She cares more about the effort and the process than the end result, and consequently, can't understand why I am getting salty.

Try thinking about your own blind spots, and that of those around you. What are you like, in terms of personality traits? Analytical or emotional? Extroverted or introverted? Consequently, what are you missing? These aren't necessarily easy questions to answer and so asking for honest opinion from friends and family could be useful – trust me, you'll be shocked at some of the things people say. In addition, I would recommend taking the Myers Briggs personality online test: it only takes 10 minutes or so but provides you with detailed intel about yourself (as well as names of celebrities with your personality type). Then take what you've learned further, attempt to explain behaviours exhibited by yourself or others. Perhaps, your *ambition* is making you appear *careless* toward family matters while you don't see that? Or maybe, you like starting things and *never really finish* them because you cannot sustain your *drive and excitement*? Take a think break.

Once you've identified your blind spots (and that of those you're in touch with on the daily) you're ready for change. You'll understand people better, you'll communicate better and you'll learn new things which were previously in the periphery of your blind spot. This is especially relevant if you consider doing a start-up – your team members must compensate for each other's blind spots. This way, a meritocratic system of selection of the best decision will flourish.

6: Be Selfish. Be Pragmatic.

Before you read into this too much, disclaimer: this isn't exactly a philosophy that a lot of authors & influencers preach (though many of them live by it). This mental principle was formulated by myself and (initially) for myself; therefore, it may be uncomfortable to implement for some of my readers.

Here's the thing: the vast majority of people you meet in life *don't care*. They don't care about you, your feelings, your thoughts, your opinions, your worries, your activities, or your financial well-being. People care about themselves and occasionally, those in their closest circle (such as family members or best friends). Everyone has an agenda they follow. Often times, if it contradicts with your wants and needs, others will not hesitate to neglect your desires in favour of their agenda. If that's something you haven't realized yet, you're not meeting enough people.

Think about someone you consider a close friend. *There is* a pragmatic, selfish reason why they are friends with you. On a good day, your friend won't realize what this reason is: he or she will just feel drawn to you inexplicably and feel loyal towards you. *But the reason is there.* Maybe it's because you're funny – you make them laugh a lot and they enjoy that. Maybe you act as their emotional swamp drain – you're a good listener and always give reconciliating advice. Or maybe you keep on stroking their ego by sucking up to them a lot. On a bad day, your friend *will* know the exact reason why they sustain this relationship and aim to exploit you consciously. Do you have a lot of Instagram followers? Or maybe a lot of money? Or connections of some sort or other? Look out for an insincere someone in your circle – they almost certainly will be using you in some form. Either way, on both "good" and "bad" days, one truth is evident: **most people don't want you for you, people want you for what you give to them.**

Now, what do you do with this devastating information? Well, first, you register it. Then you accept it as a phenomenon that occurs in *your* life and maybe look for signs of innate selfishness in the people of your circle. If you look closely, you'll find those reasons and those agendas. The most useful place to go from here is when living life in the future – bear in mind all people are selfish in some way or another.

As someone who's reading the "Capitalist Manifesto," someone who wants transformative change to their live, you should be prepared to have an agenda of your own. For instance, you want to make money. That's it. It doesn't matter what most other people think, it doesn't matter how you may appear in the eyes of society, and it doesn't matter if you're getting judged. At the end of the day, everybody is doing this anyway, but most are just a little more discrete about it. When you win on the stock market, you're bagging someone else's loss. It's "eat or get eaten."

Storytime: a man by the name of Ray Kroc was selling milkshake mixers in the 1950s. As he went from restaurant to restaurant trying to offload the mixers, he stumbled across McDonalds – a fast-food place co-owned by brothers Dick and Mac in San Bernardino, California. Having been in thousands of kitchens, Ray knew this had to be the best-run restaurant he had ever seen – the preparation and dispense of orders was done through a truly revolutionary system. Ray quit his job as a mixer salesman and began working for Dick and Mac. He saw a big opportunity for expansion.

Unfortunately, Dick and Mac were inventors much more than entrepreneurs. They were sceptical about Ray's ambitious expansion plans, they did not want to optimize costs by using pre-made milkshake powder instead of real ice cream, they were hesitant to travel and build, and broadly speaking, were happy with keeping McDonalds as it was – one single restaurant in San Bernardino. Not only that, they were getting in Kroc's way and becoming a burden. So, Ray Kroc followed his agenda regardless – through clever legal work and alteration of the business model, he essentially seized the business from the brothers, then made it a wild success. Later, he even paid a nice compensation to Dick and Mack for their initial commitment (though the amount was incomparable to that which they would have received if they stayed in the business). While the ethical motives of Raymond Kroc are questionable, he can only be applauded for living by the philosophy outlined above. He recognized people are selfish, the brothers don't care about a "big" future, and that no one is going to help him because no one cares. So, he took matters into his own hands and followed his agenda. That worked out very, very well for Mr Kroc and if it hadn't, today there would be no McDonalds.

Create and follow your own agenda. Be selfish. Achieve. If you're the type of person that wants to make *everyone* happy, try giving out free ice-creams in the park instead.

7: Plan Things

It's hard to underestimate the power of a plan. The generalized road to success goes a little like this:

1. Have a dream/vision. Make sure you're sustainably passionate about it.

2. Make a detailed plan. Set deadlines. This turns your dream into an attainable goal.

3. Execute.

4. Repeat.

While almost anyone can achieve step one (to have a dream), most people will not get beyond this stage. They will suppress their passions or find excuses not to get out of their comfort zone. But even those that do make it to step two will most likely trip up there and then. Planning things is not always easy.

In planning things, the scale in which you wish to implement this tactic is entirely up to you. You could stop at planning out your things-to-do at the beginning of each day. It can even be as little as: "There are a few emails I need to send, here they are in order of importance, so when going onto my laptop, I will spend 30 minutes doing that and only then I will allow myself to get distracted by YouTube." Or, it can be as big as "I know I want to build a tech company in the Silicon Valley, so once I graduate college, I'm going to move to San Francisco , gain experience working in a relatively developed start-up, gain useful connections, start my own thing, take it to an IPO, become a billionaire and retire by the age of 50." I'm oversimplifying here, of course, but hopefully this gives you an idea about how little or how big your plans can be.

I would recommend planning all the time and everywhere. It adds structure to both the flow of events in your life and your way of thinking. It makes you organized. Just like any other habit, it's something that can be trained and engrained into your mentality. As a bonus, planning also gives you a pleasant sense of fulfilment if you then stick to your strategy and achieve your goals.

Please avoid being that person who has written up an infinite number of incredibly audacious plans and ideas but hasn't gotten his hands down to executing any of them. Begin with small-scale plans, then scale up. Start planning!

8: *Struggle & Motivate*

We've got the vision and the passion, we've got the agenda, we've got the open-mindedness and we've got the plan. One other crucial "commodity" is commonly mentioned in self-development books – *motivation*. The things mentioned above may be sufficient to get you started, but they won't last to see you through the execution of your plans. That requires hard, tiring work. Such work requires energy which one can only source through motivation.

There are two types of motivation – the "stick" method and the "carrot" method. Both methods involve you being pushed towards the edge of your comfort zone (shown by the dashed line above) and eventually stepping out of that zone entirely to get to a new, better place. From personal experience and from what I have read, one type of motivation is marginally more effective than the other – can you guess which one?

It's the "stick." Psychologically, most humans are pre-programmed to be more driven by fear than reward. What would you rather: lose something valuable you already have or not gain something valuable you could have gained? For the majority, losing something they already have is more painful. People like to stick to the status quo. This is why "stick" motivation often proves more effective: if you don't get yourself together and act, you'll end up in the "bad place." You're motivated by fear and struggle – this gives you the energy to act and progress. This is the reason why you see so many millionaires and billionaires rising to the very top from the very bottom – their reality at the time of despair and difficulty was either at, or dangerously close to, the "bad place." They knew that if they were to do nothing, they'd end up on the streets; or in a homeless shelter; or as a family disappointment; or even in the same place they're in today five years down the line – a lack of progress over time translates to regress. Their fears (the sticks) did an excellent job at loading them with energy to work hard and excel. I personally have also found that, generally speaking, "fear of the stick" is more motivating to both myself and the people working with me than the reward of the carrot. People tend to get things done quicker and more efficiently because they're scared of catching the stick.

Do not dismiss the "carrot" motivation method quite yet though. While less people are receptive to this type of motivation, it has its own significant merits. From my own observations, people who are well motivated by "carrots" tend to be, on average, a little more intelligent than those who aren't. I think this is explained by the fact that "carrot" motivation requires a construct in the mind of the person being motivated – a distinct projection into a better future. It necessitates imagination: the person must be able to picture their carrot clearly and must recognize that this is what they want. An unclear future benefit is harder to visualize than a known present harm and, therefore, is less of a motivator. But if you do find success in "carrot" motivation, you'll find the experience much more purposeful. As opposed to the "stick," you're not running *from* something to a yet unknown *somewhere,* you're running to a very specific *somewhere* while patting yourself on the back. When starting this book, I knew immediately this was going to be a "carrot" situation. I have nothing to fear: if I don't write the "Manifesto," my life would not change for the worse, but if I do write it, my life (and hopefully, lives of my readers) will change for the better. So, when I get tired of typing all of this up, I try and picture my "carrot:" the reviews of all the people who found the "Manifesto" useful, the status of having written a book at 19 and the money from sales which I'll further donate to change people's lives. I'm running *towards,* not running *from,* and that makes my journey more cohesive and resolute. On the other hand, with studying for tests at school or university, I always tend to do everything last minute. I'm usually preoccupied with things other than studying 20-year old textbooks up until the very point where the test is right around the corner. Then, the adrenaline rush kicks in, blood starts pumping and my brain processes information at a faster-than-usual pace. I memorize the things I need to know and get my "A"s. I'm motivated by the stick – a fear of failing these darn exams.

The takeaway should be this: your best bet at succeeding in self-motivation is employing some sort of combination of the two motivation methods. Remember, the "Manifesto" falls under the "**self**-improvement" genre – this means you need to find ways of motivating *yourself* to enact advice given in this book instead of relying on an authoritative figure. I know that for me, both the "carrot" *and* the "stick" can be good motivators and, therefore, depending on the situation which requires my commitment, I consciously choose to motivate myself one way or the other. You should do the same.

P.S: on a very personal note, one of my worst fears and subsequently motivators is mediocrity. I truly don't know how much of a "stick" this would be to most readers, but one of my scariest nightmares is being *average*. To be the "average Joe," or, as some may call it, a "basic b*tch." Mediocrity is *lame*. Conventionality is *boring* and *repulsive*. Now that I think of it, this is probably why I've never liked soccer as a kid – literally every other boy in my boarding school loved it and it just seemed like such a basic interest to me, I subconsciously pushed it away. I still don't like soccer... **Failure is not the opposite of excellence, mediocrity is.**

Chapter 7:

Spending Habits

It is no accident "spending habits" supersedes "mentality" – the two are closely linked and some principles that should be employed when spending (such as rationality) have already been mentioned in the previous chapter. There are, however, a few other things to say in relation to spending which make a separate chapter worthy of attention.

People think that once you're a millionaire (and even more so, a billionaire), you can buy whatever you want without counting your money. Surely – think the "common" folk – you have so much cash, no matter how much you spend you will just never run out? This is a logical misconception – individuals who's spending never measured in millions or hundreds of thousands do not comprehend how such sums can be spent, and how on earth anyone can desire anything more. Some of the rich help entrench the "reckless" spending imagery with $450 million gold-plated yachts, Boeing Business Jets, and 12-litre champagne bottles, also giving grounded rise to dangerous socialist attitudes. In reality, things are very different.

If being rich was all about the absolute value of money you have in the bank, lottery winners from the slums would live the same as self-made millionaires. But they don't: *they go bust.* In fact, 70% of lottery winners are almost certain to declare bankruptcy within 5 years of their jackpot. They spend lavishly, go on holiday, and dispense no-interest loans to friends and family – in other words, they do everything they *think* describes how the rich live. In fact, they are missing one key bit.

Wealth is not quantitative. Wealth is not just the raw amount of assets that you own, it's your assets *relative* to your liabilities (spending). Think of it as a pot of gold – the contents of the pot are your fortune. You want your fortune to keep on growing and there is only one way of doing that: consistently put more gold *into the pot* than that you take out.

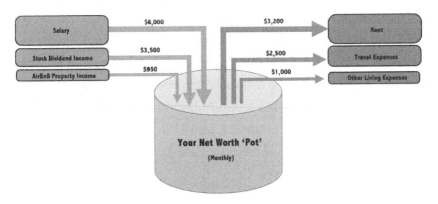

As you see above, your sources of income (or assets) in green must always exceed your income "eaters" (liabilities). As modelled, your monthly income of $10,450 after subtracting your monthly costs of $6,700 leaves you with a net positive gain of $3,750. This monthly residue can then be used to expand your income streams (such as adding another Airbnb property) or to mildly increase your expenses. Either way, ensure your "pot" is bloating. *This is the key.*

You can replace "salary" with "income from my business," "rent" with "cost of servicing my private plane," and the thousands of dollars can be replaced by millions – it makes no difference to the model's fundamental structure: Money in > Money Out.

This is all relatively basic theory though; you'd be surprised how many people abstain from living by this intuitive tactic. In the day and age of online retail, cult-crazed coffee shops, infinite diets & supplements and in-app purchases, there is *so much* dumb shit you can buy that you don't need. You don't *need* Starbucks, you don't *need* avocado toast and Acai bowls, and you don't need a "$49.99/month personalized vitamin box in custom packaging." Just be smart about these things!

In London, I travel by tube most of the time and when not, I only take UberX. I also fly economy class– a mildly stiffer 19-years-old back is totally worth the $3,000 I'm saving when not paying for business. All of this despite the fact that I can comfortably afford hiring a full-time driver to carry me around London and can hypothetically charter a private jet when I travel around Europe. There are plenty of examples of millionaires and billionaires doing things you wouldn't expect them to do: Warren Buffet never spends more than $4 on breakfast, Alice Walton (wealthiest woman in the world) drives a Ford F-150, Zuckerberg wears the same outfit almost all of the time, and my dad wears a G-Shock and owns no Rolex watches. These are smart people teaching us a lesson: if you are comfortable with your financial position, there's no need to be flashy or pretentious. Remember to be *rational* about your spending and don't betray the spending model.

ANOTHER P.S.: Debt is evil, and you (as an individual) should avoid it at all costs. Picture our "wealth" pot above: getting a credit card loan to finance your spending would be akin to punching a hole in the bottom of the pot. Not only do you lose what's already in there, you also end up continuously leaking any future income you receive into your credit hole. Your hands are tied. Same thing with student loans: by taking one out, you risk shackling yourself into steel hand-cuffs for decades to come. Some people cannot avoid student debt – for you, ask yourself whether college really will pay off for you. Is it worth the credit struggle?

If you find yourself in a situation where you need to use debt to sustain your living standards, you're in trouble. Stop and think. The solution is another income stream, not loans. The temporary relief you'll experience "affording" something with a credit card is far out-weighed by the long-run burden of your credit. Don't pay to spend. The only circumstance where using debt as an individual is justified is if you use the loaned funds to build another income stream. Even then, that's a risk. While debt in all forms should ideally be avoid-ed, if you do find yourself indebted, don't disassociate yourself as a beneficiary of "Manifesto's" principles – you *can* still build extensive wealth, but aim to prioritize paying back what you owe and putting yourself in a position where you don't have to borrow again.

Chapter 8:

To The "Crazy" Ones Building a Business

I'll start by saying I will not be giving away *all* of my best kept secrets quite yet and that is for your sake just as much as mine. I could try writing a whole book on business (or maybe even two) to add to the thousands that have been written already. I'm not going to do that: there is no time nor space for this within the "Manifesto," my expertise isn't quite there yet and frankly, if some readers really are determined to discover more of these "magical" secrets, they themselves will be able to find them. So, outlined in this chapter are just a few of the most key, most potent principles that first came to mind when I was planning what I have to say on business.

My definition of a "business" in the context of this book is truly quite broad. A "business" differs from an investment into any other asset class (such as stocks or cryptocurrencies) in that you are granted control over the life and fate of the whole asset. Bitcoin will exist regardless of whether you buy it or sell it. Oil prices will fluctuate regardless of whether you speculate on them. But a business, *your* business, is wholly dependent on the decisions you make, and it can be as big or as niche as you want it to be. You have significant – if not complete – control.

This is why starting a business is your best shot at becoming a millionaire or a billionaire. Creating, running, expanding, and sustaining a business consumes your character fully (instead of, for instance, just the analytical thinking you'd employ when picking a stock to buy), it brings out full-time dedication, emotional attachment, and powerful drive. It becomes a *lifestyle*.

It does, however, require incredibly *hard* work – when you work for yourself (or as such, your business), you have no holidays, no weekends, and no lunch breaks. No one is going to come and pick up from where you left off – you are the sole carrier of responsibility for the success (or failure) of your company. It also requires *smart* work – just working your ass off is enough for an employee, but not a business owner. Your ultimate assessment metric is not the number of hours you put in nor the amount of time you spent worrying about the company doing well: it's all about *results* your business does or doesn't bring.

Your odds of succeeding in building your own company drop down lower if you have no connections. Network is power. Knowing someone (ideally, in your business sector) that can provide guidance or offer you a useful contact can translate into millions of dollars in revenue. Believe it or not, we still live in a world of nepotism. Connections you build (or have already) can be your vital resource, the lack of which may fatally doom your chances.

I am a firm believer that owning & running a business is not for everyone. In other words, most readers should *not* do this. Aside from notable work ethic, full-time commitment, a decent idea and a team, you also need to have developed a specific way of thinking. Most people don't think in an entrepreneurial way and from what

I've seen, this isn't something that can exactly be fixed. You kind of have *it* or you **don't**. Entrepreneurial thinking is also something that can hardly be taught through textbooks and online courses because business is more of a way of life as opposed to a skill in its purest form. Instead, this way of thinking is cultivated by your upbringing, your habits and genetic predisposition to certain character traits.

Now that I've scared away the faint of heart from starting their own company, let's get down to business. Speaking of which: you need to build one! At my age, I've started three different companies: one did reasonably well, one failed completely and entirely and the third one did okay (but not good enough by my self-imposed standards). I am indeed at the very start of my journey in terms of big business, but my background, knowledge, and network have all gone to teach me valuable lessons. This chapter draws on wisdom from my personal experiences and (even more so) from experiences and ideas outlined by other incredibly successful businessmen and women.

Lesson #1: Opportunity is EVERYWHERE.

As I've said earlier in this chapter, for the purpose of this text we use quite a broad interpretation of "business." In this light especially, this first lesson is *very* true. There is a common misconception about entrepreneurship and business that you have to come up with some ground-breaking, revolutionary, transformative idea or you fail. This is wrong! The reason for this misjudgement is simple: as the general public, we often hear a lot about "revolutionary" businesses like Airbnb and hear very little about smaller scale, more mundane businesses that are in fact the driving force behind global economies. From the media's point of view, it's much more interesting to cover something edgy like renting out floor or kitchen space of your own home than it is to write about some 25-years-old British lad making six-figure income drop-shipping mugs from China. A lot of people also give in to the bias of fierce competition in business (underpinned by news we constantly hear about booming developing economies in Asia, expanding human population, etc.) but the truth is: you really don't have to have a *fundamentally* different product or service in order to do well in business.

Most business is actually pretty ordinary. A Nigerian man who buys bananas for 12c each at Point A and sells them for 20c each at Point B is *a businessman*. My 13-year old cousin selling rare Supreme Streetwear T-Shirts is *a businessman*. My father ships cargo through ports and railways – he is also a *businessman*. What I'm getting at is: you don't have to be unique in *what* you're doing but rather, special in *how* you're doing it.

Let's use the example of my younger reletive: re-selling Supreme is not unique nor revolutionary. Generically, it's actually quite a common craft with (supposedly) intense competition from "hypebeast" sellers. But a business doesn't work generically, it works specifically. If my cousin, *specifically,* find a *specific* way to sell *specific* items in a way that makes buyers flock to him instead of his competitors, he already won. He tells me his secret is the time which passes between official item release and his own re-sale listing on StockX. Whether that's true or not, I do not know, but I do see my little cousin with thick stacks of cash every now and then. Good for him – he found opportunity suitable to his lifestyle, interest, and pocket-size and so he gets rewarded.

The world is big and ever-changing. There's opportunity to create and distribute value everywhere – all you have to do is be observant and think carefully. What interests you, that you can do reasonably well, that you can also sell? Start thinking on smaller scale (such as selling Juul pods at a premium), and then move to bigger things (such as, maybe, buying under-priced tree logs in Russia and shipping them over to sell in Europe). Opportunity is everywhere!

Lesson #2: Employ Global Asymmetry.

Global asymmetry is a concept I have myself identified as unmistakably present a long while ago, yet the idea has received limited coverage by writers and gurus in the self-development & business genre. This concept is simply that of an imbalance, that is ever-present and that can be used by business people to their advantage. Asymmetry exists *everywhere*: in information, in skills, in resources, and is in fact inherent within capitalism. It even exists in nature.

First, we address the "gold" of the 21st century: information. There is now more information globally than there has ever been in the history of mankind, and this information is as accessible as ever. Despite this, the level and quality of information processed by different firms and individuals differ starkly and it is often *because of this asymmetry* that some companies are valued at trillions of dollars while others go bankrupt (or why some men are worth billions while others live on less than one dollar per day). Of course, informational imbalance is not the only cause for monetary inequality, but it certainly receives less credit than it is due.

From a consumer perspective, one would buy a MacBook over a Dell laptop thanks to *informational asymmetry*: you do not know (nor want to know) that Dells actually offer much better performance metrics, greater charge longevity, better processing speed, etc. Instead, you go with the Mac because it's Apple, or because your friends have it, or because it's seen as less nerdy and boasts a sleeker design. Apple has done incredibly well in using it's smart branding to succumb consumers to giving into informational asymmetry (and making an *irrational* decision) – so well, their *trillion-dollar* valuation is justified.

Someone always knows something you don't know! This is why, under capitalist societies we get "winners" and "losers" – and the winners unfailingly tend to have an edge in terms of information. In terms of your business, having more information (about your customers, about the market structure, about innovation or anything relevant else) than your competitor guarantees an advantageous position. The more you know (and the less your competition knows), the better your strategy can be.

Asymmetry doesn't only exist in information: it's also present in resource (such as raw materials or human capital) and skills possessed by different workers. Some are out there trying to fight this asymmetry and "level out the playing field." I'm just out there taking advantage of it, having accepted its imminence. You should do the same. If you manage to get an edge in skill, knowledge or specific information relevant to a distinct situation, you will already be a few steps ahead of the game. Use this as a mental trick, make it your principle! ***Asymmetry presents opportunity.***

Broadly speaking, this lesson is about getting an edge. This also ties back to generic and specific knowledge mentioned in Chapter 2 and extends those concepts further: you need to know *more* in order to benefit from asymmetry, you need to possess skills which put you steps ahead of others. I do acknowledge this lesson is of a generic nature, but if you put this ideology in the forefront of your mind, you'll find yourself making decisions (relevant to your specific business) that employ global asymmetry to your advantage.

Lesson #3: Do not create a problem to solve it.

From personal experience investing in Venture Capital (and, for that matter, starting my own company), I can assert that one of the most common mistakes in start-ups is creating a non-existent problem. Let's revert to basics a little.

The aim of every start-up company, fundamentally, is to provide a solution to a problem. It is to *sell* the solution to businesses or consumers and make money while doing so. Unfortunately, many business founders fall into the trap of creating a problem themselves – one which seems to be well resolved by their "incredible" invention. To give you an example: a while back, I was approached by a Silicon Valley start-up which claimed to be the next big internet thing. The company allowed users to organize their articles, videos, and other online content in a virtual room, essentially creating a browser within a browser. They claimed to have conducted online surveys which confirmed their product was in demand, raised millions (largely from inexperienced investors) and developed the software technology for their product. The company was a total failure. No one wanted to use their "solution" because there was no "problem" of using a normal browser for content consumption in the first place.

When considering a business idea, make sure to ask yourself: "Does this solution resolve a *real* problem?" and "Is this something that people would *really* be willing to pay for?" If the business pitch in question is one of your own, be aware that your answer will be subjective. Your ego is your blind spot – you are more likely to think you have a great business idea if you are the one that thought if it. It's best to get a second opinion from someone that you know will be brutally honest with you. Even better if that someone is somewhat qualified (like a business owner or an experienced investor) to give you great advice. Having said all that though, 20 years ago people would call letting a stranger sleep in your house on an inflatable mattress an insane business idea. Today, Airbnb has a $35 billion valuation. The point is that valued judgement and intuition are your best friends.

Lesson #4: Have a passion

Steve Jobs, Bill Gates, and Jack Ma all (more or less) do a good job at explaining why having passion as a business owner is so crucial – it's definitely worth looking at some videos of them talking about it on YouTube. In essence, though, it's because starting a business requires *so much* work and energy, it'd be impossible to persevere without passion. Unlike anything else, entrepreneurship will captivate you entirely – you won't really have "off-hours" or weekends where you can completely disengage yourself from the company. It's always on your mind (or in the back of it). You're working on it all the time, even by just thinking about it. At its core, entrepreneurship is the product of vision and passion, not vice versa.

Here's the thought process a lot of wannabe entrepreneurs wrongly go through:

1. I think entrepreneurship sounds cool and I can fit it into my lifestyle. Totally sounds better than "unemployed!"

2. I've decided I'm going to start my own company.

3. I'm deciding on what exactly that company should be, I'm not too sure. Probably something... Fun?

4. I've kind of made up my mind. Let's get going and try to accumulate required resource.

5. I'm going to develop my passion and entrepreneurial "drive" as I go.

Here's the optimal thought process the minority go through:

1. I have a vision. I find a problem and I'm keen to resolve it. I think about what I need to succeed. I am **passionate.**

2. I consider the options and opportunities for finding a solution. I consult knowledgeable people about my idea.

3. I realize I'm going to build a company. I build a good team – our visions will align.

4. I accumulate all other required resource (such as capital). I'm off to build and expand my company.

See the difference? The better approach *starts* with finding a problem and developing passion, while the worse *ends* with it.

If you are starting a company because you think it's cool, or because it's fashionable, or because you're unemployed, you're doomed to fail. It's also worth saying that often times, a passion *cannot be artificially induced.* Much like entrepreneurial-style thinking, it either develops or it doesn't. If it does, you'll have no doubt. Note that you're more likely to have a passion for something you already have an inclination to (such as fashion, technology or art) so it is worth scanning those fields first and foremost

Lesson #5: People

The importance of people in business cannot be underestimated. You're selling to people, you're buying from people and most importantly, you're working with people. Business fail, also, because of people. In fact, if you can't get the right team sorted for your business, you might as well stop wasting your time. I've learned this the hard way: in one of the start-ups I created, I've put someone who was more suited to be a regular employee (i.e. someone that is only good at completing explicitly clear and simple tasks set to them by someone else) in an executive position; position which required a proactive approach and a little bit of unconventional thinking to go with it; a position which should emphasize *result over process*. I told myself that he will be able to develop those necessary thinking skills as we go, and that with my guidance his incompetence will not be a threat to the business' ultimate success. I was very, very wrong and paid for my mistake accordingly – this played a major role in the start-up's ultimate failure.

I would seriously recommend taking the Myers-Briggs personality test to every business founder, and make potential employees or partners take the test too. It gives valuable insights about the way people think and consequently, what you may be lacking on your team. For instance, you may find out that almost all your leadership positions are filled with extroverted "feelers" – people who rely on emotions or intuition to guide their decisions. While this isn't a bad thing in itself, it may be worth considering adding some introverted "analysts" – those, perhaps, with less charisma, but with a more analytical frame of mind.

Broadly, just keep in mind that business is about people. People who make mistakes, people who have different values (and consequently, would give into different persuasion techniques), and people who have varied views. No businessman is impartial to his/her background and personal biases. If you remember this and get good at reading people (this goes back to our point about using information to your advantage), your odds of success will surge significantly.

Lesson #6: Theorize by Theory, Practice by Practice.

Communism may be good in theory, but terrible in practice. Theoretically, it delivers equality of opportunity and outcome, abundance of resource accessible to all, it eradicates income and wealth inequality, and minimizes waste of scarce resource. Practically though, communism delivers a vicious, oppressive, totalitarian state, mass hunger, murder, riots, and dead economies. In fact, communism (alongside fascism) is probably *the* worst experiment of humanity on humanity, and the leading ideological cause of death in the 20th century. This goes to show the difference between theory and practice.

So how is this a business lesson? Well, when I dove into my second start-up, the idea looked exceptional in theory. We were going to capitalize on the growing trend of the sharing economy and rent out luxury clothing and accessories to people who can't afford them for a fraction of the retail price. When I was in boarding school, friends would often come up to me and ask to borrow a Gucci T-Shirt or some Valentino sneakers for the night, offering £20 or so in exchange. This seemed to validate our business concept. Furthermore, prior to spending cash on building required infrastructure for the rentals (website, warehouse, delivery system, etc.), we conducted an online survey targeted to our specific audience – young men in Britain. Out of the 60,000 people surveyed, 34,000 said they would be interested in our services and would be willing to pay. That is, in theory. In practice, that number was less than 50 people. Less than 50 people ended up paying! We were baffled – we tried one-time rentals as well as subscription services, we tried all sorts of marketing, we invested in quality design and packaging and still for nothing. We knew for a fact exactly the same service in the luxury segment exists for women and is actually doing quite well. What were we doing wrong? Turns out, we violated *two* lessons outlined in this chapter; one: we created a solution for a market that wasn't really there and two: we heavily relied on theory to inform what we do in practice. Boys simply aren't a market we thought they were. But because we were so caught up on our ingenious theory, we left ourselves very little space for manoeuvre. We couldn't suddenly change our target audience or company concept and so I decided to shut the whole thing down and invest my time in other, more profitable ventures.

The takeaway here is: as a start-up founder, whatever you envision and theorize will probably differ from what happens in real life. You will go through a process of constant iteration, processing information given to you by your market and altering your idea here and there. I struggle to think of a start-up that got it right straight away – even Airbnb (probably the "craziest" business idea of this century) had to change things along the way. Bearing in mind this discrepancy between theory and practice, make sure you build your company in a way which allows it to adapt and evolve easily so it can deliver the best possible result.

Lesson #7: Shit Happens.

You knew this one was coming. If you didn't, welcome to the daily world of business founders – things tend to turn sour from time to time. In fact, it is likely that at the very start of your journey, things will be *consistently* sour. That's okay – we already know that failures are good *so long* as you learn from them and improve.

Picture this: you've had an idea. You've found a great partner. You raised some money. You've hired good people. You're incredibly excited, but…things are not exactly going according to plan. People around you are not manifesting your vision as you see it. Perhaps they don't even fully understand your vision and are in this for the money. Things take longer than expected. You and your partner are frustrated and argue often. Even an investor that promised more funding has just pulled out. Pretty damn miserable, isn't it?

As unpleasant as all this sounds, it's reality. No pain - no gain. The best thing to do when "shit happens" (and incidentally, the opposite of what the vast majority of people do) is not to "bundle" your troubles. Instead of thinking "it's all going wrong, this start-up's a failure, I'm a failure, this will never work, etc." treat each problem that emerges individually. Think this way: "It's not *all* going wrong, only A, B and C. I know how to solve A, that's relatively easy and not truly a big problem. B is a little tougher, but I will speak with my employees and decide on how to address this issue. Lastly, I really don't know how to solve C, so I will go to my mentor for advice and see what he says." This methodical approach stops you from being overwhelmed in troubled times and allows you to keep your eyes on the prize. It's simple, folks: if you have a problem you *can* solve, you *will* solve it. If a problem emerges which there is *nothing* you can do about, you *shouldn't spend time* worrying about it.

Lesson #8: Sales is King. Profit is Queen.

In recent times, it has become fashionable for start-ups not to make money - this stems from the Silicon Valley, where losing money from operations is still seen by many as a good thing. With some companies that prioritize establishing a dominance within their market (think Tesla), a sustained strategy of operating at a loss is somewhat justifiable, I would argue that the majority of start-ups misunderstand (and consequently, misuse) the idea. All the time, we hear about internal company culture, decision-making processes, exceptional teams, and other secondary aspects of a business – sometimes, investors are even fed straight-up nonsense like Neumann's made-up "community-adjusted EBITDA" metric. While *some* of those things are important, many founders seem to lose the main focus – *no business has ever survived without sales.* You can have great company culture and a fantastic partnership between two, or three, or four bright founders, but if you're not getting sales all of that means *nothing*.

When going into business, you have to know what you're selling, to whom you're selling, why you're selling, and *how* you're selling. If you overemphasize other aspects of a start-up (you often hear app founders say "we are not worried about monetization, all we care about is our user count") you drift away from building a business. You're now building something else. All this, by the way, is not to say you should cut corners on product development, user experience or, for that matter, anything else: all I'm saying is that you should always keep your **prime target** in sight (which is, if you're a businessman, *to sell*). Remember – "**sales is king.**"

If sales is king, then profit is queen. Why? Because (historically) the queen has been subordinate to the king and only gained her powers once the kings lost his. The first-ever (self-proclaimed) queen of England – Mary I – began her reign thanks to circumstance: her brother Edward died of tuberculosis in 1553. Similarly, profit is secondary to sales in its importance and comes into play at a later stage, and yet its presence or absence can be life-changing. Making sales is not easy, but it's also not *too* hard. Making profit is a whole different story: there are tons of companies out there that deliver great big sale volumes but struggle to make a profit. Since the ultimate goal of every business (especially its shareholders) should be profit, lack thereof can get very problematic. Once again, the Silicon Valley is to blame – too many companies nowadays disregard profit almost entirely and give out (largely) empty promises of grasping the biggest market share. Profit is even less fashionable than sales!

Look, regardless of whether you would reinvest all profits into R&D or spend them all on shareholder dividends, you're going to need them sooner or later. The sooner the better – you're in business for the money. **Profit is queen.**

At its core, this lesson is about planning and ties back neatly with my seventh "Mentalist Lesson" outlined in Chapter 6. As a business founder, do not forget the importance of sales and profit. You need not aim to excel in either from day one (that's barely a realistic target), but you should have a clear understanding of how you will bring about both when the time is right.

Lesson #9: Decisions & Stakes

Business is also about decisions. All the time. I've already praised *"Principles"* as a decision-making guide for life in general, but for an entrepreneur especially, this book should be gospel. As it is generally recommended to start a venture with a partner(s) (as opposed to by yourself), you will need to devise a process guiding your collective decisions. This is where stakes come in: your ownership percentage of the company, especially at early stages of its development, will inevitably translate into the extent of power you will enjoy. From personal experience, equal shares (and thus, equal executive power) leads to conflict and gridlock sooner or later. I theorize that your best bet is to have one majority stakeholder with ultimate decision-making rights, and a minority stakeholder(s) – perhaps, with the right of veto or other pre-determined arrangements to enable exercise of executive action. Look at Google – the corporation's wild success made several men billionaires, but if we assess the exact stakes of each, we see the following:

- Larry Page (co-founder) owns 20 million Class B & 20 million Class C shares and is worth $55 billion

- Sergey Brin (president, co-founder) owns 19 million Class C shares and 35,300 of Class A and B shares, he's worth $54 billion

- Eric Schmidt (early ex-CEO) owns 1.2 million Class C shares, 1.2 million Class B shares (and other), he's worth $13 billion

See how Brin and Page benefitted in (almost) exactly the same way from Google's success and amassed $55 billion fortunes, yet Page (due to his marginal majority) had the edge in terms of decision-making during Google's early days. Would Google have been able to reach such heights had their ownership stakes been exactly the same, or would their strategical disagreements lead to a Mexican standoff? That's certainly something to think about.

With this said, there are also several examples of exceptional businesses that were built with equal ownership stakes between the founders (my father's port business is one of such). In this case, there must be clear distinctions between respective fields of action of each executive, and ideally, differentiated personalities. If all the founders find themselves doing the same things, while also being *too* similar or *too* different in character, there will inevitably be a clash sooner or later, and that can really kill the business.

Lastly, there are also cases where entrepreneurs have done much better alone, instead of splitting ownership and power between partners. For some, vesting executive power in themselves only has rid them of hefty bureaucratic hassles and power struggles and enabled them to build a functional business without such obstacles. It all depends on your personality and the business that you're in. So, ask yourself: are you a team player? Is the business filed you're entering more suited for a partnership structure or are you better off by yourself?

Regardless of which path you choose, one thing's for certain: you will need to make decisions and in order to make good ones, you'll have to devise a protocol. Use prioritized criterion, devise a set of principles, follow them. Make the best decisions possible. Succeed.

A few other things to think about:

1. Starting is one of the hardest parts. Finding money, resources and the right people is *hard*. So, be creative! I could try and teach you what to do, but my advice would never be precise enough for your exact situation. Moreover, if you cannot resolve these issues yourself, you need to rethink whether you should be an entrepreneur. No spoon-feeding here, folks.

2. Fundraising can be a challenge. Or it can be a blessing! It depends. As a founder, it is almost inevitable that at some stage you will have to look for funds from external investors – those can be individuals (such as Angel investors who register in online groups and wait for a quality start-up to ask them for money) or organizations (like Venture Capital firms of varying size). Fundraising as a topic most certainly deserves more in-depth coverage which I aim to provide in one of my later works or bonus packs – for now though, keep this in mind: *you need to carefully assess all the offers on your table (both from organizations and individuals) and make an informed choice, bearing in mind the long term consequences.* You don't want to give away too much control over your company, especially not at an early stage of its development. The valuation of your company, to which you agree, should also be fair and adequate. Remember, investors will always try and push the valuations down to snatch a bigger stake. Don't inflate your valuation (though this can be tempting) too excessively or you'll end up standing in the shoes We-Work (whose plumped up $50 billion valuation plummeted to less than $5 billion) is standing in right now. Make sure

you always have a legal advisor who can look into all the intricacies of fundraising offers to avoid nasty surprises or unfair terms later down the line.

3. Keep in mind: you will need to scale. Once you get your first sales, you'll most probably need to change a few things in order to grow your business. This is called scaling, and it is also *hard* (though the extent of this varies on what business you're in). When going into a venture, *consider scalability* – an app is much easier to scale than a manufacturing firm.

4. Ask yourself the following questions all the time and record how (if at all) your answers change; how big do you want to grow? Are you willing to sacrifice profits and personal compensation for the foreseeable future for the sake of building a massive company 20 years down the line, or is that too much to ask? Are you better off expanding or staying relatively small? Are you willing to give up your control over the company in exchange for a pile of immediate cash? There are no general right or wrong answers to each of these questions, but there will be right and wrong ones in *your specific situation*. Again, rationality, prioritization, and advice from competent others are your best friends here.

5. Luck comes to those who make themselves lucky. Best of luck!

Chapter 9:

Gurus Exposed

Imagine reading twenty or so superb business books, investing in a beanie and a quality public speaking course, subscribing to "Charisma on Command" on YouTube (a channel I highly applaud, by the way) and finally starting a "motivational" Instagram account. You've just made Gary Vee, or Tai Lopez, or Grant Cardone. There are too many of such "gurus" on social media nowadays to name them all, but the vast majority of them have one thing in common: they're all incredibly good at putting on a convincing façade.

People love them. Some even go so far as to swear by their content and claim their influence has been "life-changing." This is why my scepticism about the work of the so-called "gurus" (and, frankly, disaffection towards most of them) is classed as unjustified "unpopular opinion" by many of my friends.

Let me be clear: *most* of the things they say and preach are not wrong. Some of their pointers are actually really good advice! Want to know why? Because they come straight from the *books written by actual businessmen* - people who have *really* done it. Yet these books are in plain sight – I list many of them in the "Special Mentions" section of the "Manifesto," while principally worthy ones are referenced throughout the entirety of my writing.

These people are *salesmen and showmen* much more than they are *businessmen*. They are dependent on your views and the attention you pay them is quite literally their wage. They wrap up their "revolutionary" motivational pitches (sourced from more competent others) in nice packaging, posing in front of rented Ferrari's making you think their "Get Rich Quick & Free Through Dropshipping" audiobook is what you need in life. I really don't think it is!

As surprising as this may sound, if you are a successful businessperson (especially a young one) that is in charge of several profitable companies, guess what you'd probably be doing with your time? That's right, *running a business*. Not trying to convince a bunch of teenagers on Instagram to "Like and Subscribe." A businessman does business. A pretend businessman does Instagram.

Stop worshipping these people! The amount of times I've seen the likes of Gary Vee compared as equal to the likes of Bill Gates is outrageous. Let's wake up: they do not even stand close. "Gurus" are smart about their presentation and are good at monetizing their fame, but that's about it. They have not invented anything new. Hence, you are much better off sourcing your knowledge from authentic entrepreneurs and while they may not be on Instagram, their writing is far more valuable and legitimate. Charlie Munger's multi-billion-dollar fortune is not dependent on whether you buy his book. Neither is Peter Thiel's or Richard Branson's. But Gary Vee's is – he feeds off your screen time. Why is it that none of these notoriously "successful" mentors are anywhere to be seen on Forbes?

This has certainly been the "saltiest" chapter of the "Manifesto" but make no mistake: I hold no grudge against Gary, nor do I see him as my competition. Furthermore, I do acknowledge that his advice has changed some people's lives for the better and reached audiences otherwise unreachable. I simply am convinced that there is way too much attention being paid to the wrong people, and way too little to the right ones. If you still choose to consume their "recycled" content having read this chapter, consume it with a grain of salt.

Chapter 10:

Big Things for the Future

Nobody really knows what the future will look like. Quite thought-provoking is the fact that most people see themselves as *subjects* of their future – in other words, *something* (like flying cars, or microchip implants, or colonies on Mars) will happen whilst humans will *just be there*, and by inertia become a part of that something when it is realized. This, however, is a big fallacy because our "future" is not nearly as impartial to human activity as most make it out to be. Sure, visionaries with abundant resource (such as Elon Musk) will most likely have more impact on the future of mankind than your average Starbucks barista, but then again, you can find examples of figurative "baristas" that later suddenly became figurative Elon Musk's. *You just never know who, where, and when will have the biggest impact on the course of our history.* This is why I champion an approach that's very different from *being a subject* – I believe the **future is just what you make it to be**. Innovations and breakthroughs almost never come about randomly (aside from rare exceptions like the discovery of penicillin or the law of gravity). They happen deliberately, and especially so in the 21st century. This means *someone is actively out there*, working on something, building, trying, improving, modifying, disrupting, and **innovating.**

From this, follows the idea that we, as capitalists trying to take advantage of the "explosive" new things that will emerge in the years to come, can make *educated guesses about what trends* will be the "the next internet" or "the next industrial revolution." Thus, I will use the first segment of this chapter to present you with my very own "educated guesses" about such trends and I am sure a lot of competent investors out there will agree with the tendencies I have identified. Before we dive in, I want you to read the first sentence of this chapter again and keep that sentence in mind when reading my "trend guesses" below. The way of things in each respective field of "novelty and innovation" will most likely end up very different to what we envision now. Humans will not be replaced by robots (though that is what many sceptics now fear). We will not have Hyperloop soon transport people at 1200km/h (though that is what we are now promised) and actually, it will most likely be cargo (since human bodies can't really withstand such rapid acceleration). We also will most probably never find ourselves in an "AI-out-of-control-Skynet-Terminator" situation (unless someone deliberately develops such destructive networks). The point of all this is that any speculation about *detail* of the future made now is obsolete and almost certainly incorrect. Think of it this way: I can tell you whether our ship is generally going North, East, South, or West but I cannot accurately predict our exact direction bearings. Nonetheless, if some manifesto readers take *an educated guess* that we are heading North, they will (like myself) reap reward in being the ones feeling nice and warm in their coats once we arrive. Those who make no such guesses and thus pack *neither* coats *nor* swimming shorts (thereby choosing to be a subject) will be left out no matter whether we end up North or South.

The "elephant in the room" amongst industries set to explode is Artificial Intelligence. This touchy topic comes with a lot of irrational fears, heated public debates, expressed distaste from manual labour workers, faked-up-hype, and tulipomania. I wouldn't even class AI as *an industry* in the classical sense of the word – AI is more like a philosophy scripted in code; an approach applicable *across* industries. But what even is AI? Is singularity (or consciousness) of a machine ever even possible? Will AI cause unemployment? Should workers in enterprises such as Mc-Donalds and Walmart fear complete and total automation? Can AI be ethical? Will AI once become smarter than humans in every single way?

While I can provide an opinionated response to each of all of the above questions, and while I could write a good few dozen pages on AI (which I am tremendously passionate about), I would strongly encourage a show of research initiative. With something so new, so young and so ambiguous as AI, you should really try to form your own opinions. I may publish a separate work on this topic some time down the line, but for now, I'm saving my words and your time and force myself to cut to the chase: how can the readers of my "Manifesto" capitalize on the trend of AI? First off, here's a gentle reminder: you need to be *specifically knowledgeable* about any field or trend you wish to cash in on.

What is AI? What is machine learning? How did AI come about? What is it being used for today? Who is responsible for pioneering in the field of AI? Which publicly traded stocks are exposed to AI? Which AI companies (or departments) are hiring? What AI start-ups have made a lot of noise recently? Which failed? Why?

I like to think I know the answers to these questions – now so should you. Regardless of whether you find employment at Google's AI marketing division, or whether you invest in an AI stock, or make an AI start-up, or even just gain knowledge about AI, *you will benefit.* This thing is big, and it will keep getting bigger – it will affect your life sooner or later and in one way or another. You better be prepared – or be subjected.

From an investment perspective specifically (since this is prioritized in the Manifesto), I would just say this: once you understand the basic principles of AI, you should understand how it benefits the company you are investing into. It is not uncommon for companies to exploit the hype built around upcoming trends to pump up their valuation and make a claim like "we have developed revolutionary AI technology which will help us boost sales immensely!" If the company cannot clearly articulate why AI technology is beneficial to their business model, or even what that technology exactly is, beware – this is most probably a fad. AI *can* be revolutionary, but just like every new development, it's still going through a constant iterative process. It should make sense to you, as the investor, how AI helps or doesn't help. Don't get hooked on false or exaggerated declarations.

My next big trend guess follows on nicely from AI – it is the "Internet of Things" (IoT). This has made less noise than AI and for good reason – the IoT as an industry isn't really there yet and its applications are far less prominent than that of AI. The concept truly is fascinating: we have made internet to connect people, now let's make internet to connect things. Let's have your Nespresso machine talk to your alarm clock that in turn talks to your phone which then fires up your car. If objects we use on a daily basis can communicate to each other, they can optimize our living standards to previously unwitnessed extents, and they can greatly elevate our convenience and save us tons of time.

At this stage though, IoT is an idea much more than it is a product, and the lion's share of the value it can unlock is yet to be found. Once again, everyone likes the general notion, but no one truly knows how to use it or what to make of it. But this is changing. Therefore, the earlier you jump on this train in some way or another, the better. As a field, IoT is definitely worth researching and while you may stumble across conflicting or plain wrong information online, getting a general sense of the space is invaluable. If a start-up founder asked me which "next big thing" could bring him a billion-dollar fortune, the Internet of Things would be *very* high up on my list.

With respect to investment potential, IoT is even more hazy than AI. The latest theme which dominates the IoT narrative is satellites – companies are building and launching them, promising to erect (and some, even monopolize) the network supporting IoT transmission frequencies. We are building infrastructure to make IoT work, while we should ideally be placing more of an emphasis on the question: "What exactly are we going to use this for and how will it be profitable?" I personally see a bit of a dissonance here which only goes to further underline how early are the "early days" of IoT. But anyhow, with most of my readers probably classed as *retail* investors, I will say that IoT at this point in time is something difficult to capitalize on. Unless you have access to (and capital for) venture capital deals that grant you IoT exposure, your only bet is the "high-street" tech companies like Google. They will certainly make sure not to miss out on the IoT trend and so you could just buy into their stock – the question is, with something like Google, will their participation in this industry reap enough result for substantial stock price growth? I do not know.

All in all, I would just recommend that everybody keeps an eye on the Internet of Things. Read about it. *Know* about it. The technology is great and once the industry is mature enough, serious money is to be made. How exactly you participate in IoT is up to you, but you will most certainly hear more about it in your life. I advise you: listen and be prepared.

Another thing to keep an eye on is cryptocurrency. Cryptocurrency has probably received the most media coverage out of all my "trend guesses," and it was in fact the media that played a substantial role in causing bitcoin price spikes in 2018. There was hype and there was a bubble. You'd see taxi drivers and restaurant waiters buying bitcoin and telling their friends and family to do the same. A prolific example of 21st-century tulipomania! The price peaked at just under $20k in early January 2018, then crashed down hard. People ended up in debt and those who bought in at the very last moments have lost fortunes. Further amplified by predictable global government scepticism of cryptocurrency, the sentiment around bitcoin has changed from very bullish to very bearish, and we entered the so-called "crypto-winter." Instagram comments from the unknowledgeable masses turned from "Bitcoin is the future of money" into "Bitcoin is a scam." In my eyes, neither of those statements are true.

Sure, the vast majority of "coins" that currently exist will be worth nothing sooner or later. Yes, there have been a lot of scams and frankly, faith in digital currency has been abandoned by many. Investors don't know which coins to buy and which ones to sell. But a similar scenario has happened before…

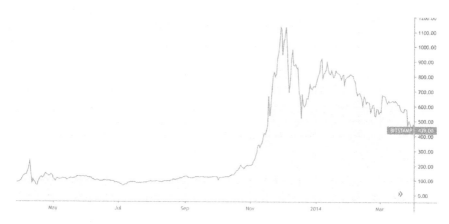

The surge above looks just like 2018. Except that it's not: what you see here is bitcoin price movements (a 10x increase in a matter of months) **in 2013**, when circumstances (at their core) weren't too different from that of 2018. People heard about it, people read about, people spoke about it, and people bought it. From there, it's exponential.

The truth of the matter is: you can find several other periods in bitcoin's trading history whereby a parabolic move upwards is followed by an equally parabolic tumble downwards. So, the important conclusion here is: bitcoin's price movements can be called *cyclical*. Up. Down. Further up. Down. Even further up. Down again... While all of this price volatility is *consistently* accompanied with optimistic agitation or pessimistic despair, bitcoin *consistently* keeps making higher highs. Mark my words; there will be a time when, once again, the hype (perhaps triggered by crypto-favourable legislation of a major government or institutional adoption) will propel bitcoin prices to pleasant highs.

The world of money is changing, and we are positively moving towards a cashless society. The "future of money" is digital! With that said, the "future of money" is also probably not Bitcoin (which I like to call the "myspace" of cryptocurrency) in the long run. The "Digital Currency 2.0" will take Bitcoin's core features and develop them to extents required for mass adoption. That "2.0" could be Telegram's new TON project, or Facebook's Libra, or even a government-sponsored scheme. One way or another, **people will use cryptocurrency**.

In terms of investment prospects for the foreseeable future, what I like to say to people is *"If you believe in cryptocurrency as an asset class and as an ideology, you believe in Bitcoin for the next three to five years."* As the pioneer of the space and the coin with 66% market dominance, bitcoin will rise in price when positive developments in the space occur. Even if it won't be around many years down the line, it can bring you decent returns in the nearer future so consider buying one of its frequent dips.

Aside from Bitcoin, I would advise retail investors and beginners in the field to steer quite clear of "altcoins" (such as Ethereum, Ripple, Tron, and others) because they all more or less follow Bitcoin's patterns – it's safer and easier for you to just stick with BTC. If, however, you find yourself doing extensive research about altcoins and feel that you are competent enough to make an informed bet with one of them, by all means go ahead. Also, keep an eye on "big-boy" projects (especially Telegram's profound network which I've invested into) and examine the possibility of investing when they are made available to the general public on exchanges.

On a more personal note: I was just 14 when I entered this space, began meeting people and learning things about this wonderful new technology. Cryptocurrency was the first-ever investment that made me seriously large profits and provided invaluable connections along the way. It was also, for a long, long time, the largest asset class in my portfolio. Thus, I have developed a bit of an affection to cryptocurrency and I sure do know a heck of a lot about it. I'm aware that many readers would view the space as "scammy" and difficult which is why I'm contemplating creating a separate piece of work dedicated entirely to cryptocurrency. Readers, please let me know by email, through my website or my Instagram page if that is something you would be interested in. VIRES IN NUMERIS!

The penultimate major "trend guess" is cannabis. Legalization and decriminalization of marijuana across the whole world (led by the United States and Canada) coupled with extensive medical research highlighting benefits of the drug had led to tremendous industry growth. In America, there are now talks to legalize marijuana on a federal level (thereby in all states), and Germany's cannabis user numbers are expected to reach one million in just a few years. Europe will, for sure, follow suit after the US and legislate on marijuana extensively very soon. The world is going to get high (or at least, highER)!

Here, once again, investors lived through a lot of hype, bloated company valuations and quite frankly, yet another bubble.

I personally follow a certain codex with my investments and have thus far steered clear of cannabis altogether (as well as guns, alcohol and gambling) but my connections in this space are vast. I speak with pioneers of the cannabis industry frequently and deem myself qualified to project what my friends have told me about prospects in marijuana.

Will the industry expand significantly? Yes. Will we see further legalization on a global scale? Yes. Are valuations of publicly-traded cannabis companies justified? For the most part, no. They are way too expensive (if we consider the modest earnings, they deliver against their stock prices) and for many of them, the only way to go is down. At this moment, I would **steer clear** from buying public stock of the vast majority of US & Canada cannabis companies (unless you have very good understanding & experience within this segment). From this follows the logical conclusion that, in order to benefit from the growth that is to be experienced by the cannabis industry, you either have to have access to private equity / VC deals which offer more adequate valuations and companies with more profitable business models *or* (what I would assume applies to most of my readers) you should just *work* in this space. You could, having researched the opportunities, create your own start-up. Or maybe you can work in someone else's start-up (and try negotiating some shares for yourself as pay). You could also find a job at one of the "weed giants" such as Tilray and work your way up. Marijuana companies are hiring!

Regardless of what path you choose in marijuana (if any), if you choose now, you will still be amongst those who boarded the weed train early (and got greater rewards). One truth is self-evident: if you want to capitalize on this trend, think about shifting from a cannabis industry consumer to a cannabis industry producer (or, even better, balance both!).

My final big "trend guess" is e-commerce. Increasingly, small and medium-sized enterprises (SMB's) as well as individuals *sell online*. Many would probably assume I'm about to start talking Amazon here, and while it is undoubtedly the e-retail "monster," that assumption is not entirely correct. Here's the thing: you can sell *on* Amazon, but you can't sell *with* Amazon. They have an established code of business, set-in-stone fee structures and concrete rules – you can upload your product onto Amazon, you can set the price and pay for the ads, but your product is still selling on Amazon.com amongst millions of other products. I'm talking about a different kind of e-commerce – I'm talking Shopify. This Canadian gemstone of a company I've found (and bought) three years ago differs from Amazon in that it lets sellers build their very own online stores using its intuitive website construction tools and convenient seller mechanisms (including simplification of delivery processes, stock management, etc.). This grants sellers freedom for their own design & personal touch, price setting unaffected by Amazon's sellers and algorithms, special promotions otherwise unmanageable, amongst many other things. Shopify makes it easy and convenient to build and run your very own, fully functional online store and consequently, erodes Amazon's position as the number one go-to for SMB's.

If you want to invest in e-commerce, consider joining me amongst the shareholders of Shopify. It trades on both the Toronto and the New York stock exchanges and is thus easily available to almost all my readers. Be informed of the risk: it does, of course, face some competition from companies like Magento and Amazon (maybe more so later down the line), but remember Shopify has been one of the fastest -growing companies over the last five years, both in terms of revenue and stock price. They've also got a great executive team and (I can attest) fantastic company culture. I'm very, very bullish.

With respect to other investment potential within e-commerce, I think it's actually worth giving Amazon some limelight. It is not poised for as much growth as Shopify (largely because it is already *so* big) but in my opinion, Jeff Bezos is the best businessman of the 21ˢᵗ century who gives little reason to doubt his abilities. Amazon – the largest e-retailer in the world – will grow more, and so will its stock price. Whether the phenomena responsible for this growth will be "e-commerce" in the classical meaning of the term, or an accompanying entity such as Amazon Web Services, the end result is all the same: more money for Bezos' empire and his shareholders. Do you want to be one of them?

Honorary mentions shortlisted from my major trend guesses are Fintech (especially small, non-traditional new banks like N26, Revolut and Monzo) and Microchips (with companies like Nvidia and Intel manufacturing hardware that in turn enables progress for trends such as cryptocurrency, AI, and IoT). Both of these are definitely worth looking into – consider whether possibilities await you in these growing spaces, either career-wise, as an investor, or as a start-up founder.

To wrap this chapter up, here's a metaphor: the year is 1992 and I have just told a bunch of people that the internet is going to generate trillions of dollars in value within the next 25 years. Some people listened, entered the space and then became Elon Musk (PayPal), Jack Dorsey (Twitter), Jeff Bezos (Amazon), Reid Hoffman (LinkedIn) and Mark Zuckerberg (Facebook) – all of whom are multi-billionaires. Others stayed in safe and "foolproof" industries such as oil and now no one knows the names of those others because most of them are nobodies.

The year is 2020 and I've just told you about upcoming trends that can be as big as the internet. Which group of people will you be income 2045?

Epilogue:

This, ladies and gentlemen, is it. This is my version of the "Golden Snitch," the "Silver Spoon" as such - perhaps imperfect and fragmentary at times, but I release it with a sense of fulfilment and hope. If you have read the "Manifesto" in its entirety, I congratulate and thank you, and truly hope you have extracted some value from this book.

As I have said before, your feedback is important to me. Please do not hesitate to reach out with questions also – I leave all contact details on the next page. My current state of affairs does not allow me to promise to write more literature or provide *daily* content on my social media platforms, but I do commit to continue dispensing value. Whether it be in the form of blog posts, articles or online products (or all of the above), I do not yet know, but I pledge to project my voice. When need be, I will discuss, expand on and update the concepts mentioned in the "Manifesto" and (judging by overwhelming demand expressed in the preliminary feedback we have collected) I will also be preparing a more specific portfolio guidance with live updates. I, therefore, ask and recommend that readers follow updates on my platforms and the website.

In an unlikely choice of topic to conclude the "Capitalist Manifesto," I want to talk about *miracles*. A man of pragmatism and rationality, I nonetheless believe in their existence. In fact, I have myself encountered a "miracle" (in the classical sense of the word) which I now briefly recollect.

The episode occured in a small monastery town that stands in rural Russia. In charge of the monestary was a priest who took great care in looking after the church, the garden with an apple orchard, the citizens of the village (a lot of whom he knew personally), and most importantly, his beloved cat called Omnibus. Omnibus was, to be frank, a nightmare – he would constantly run off to wonder, hide and get himself into trouble in various ways, but the inconveniences he caused were all selflessly forgiven by the monk. One day, the troublesome feline made the fatal decision to climb a very tall and very thin young tree in the church garden, and, as expected, ran into trouble trying to get down. The tree was young and had just began to blossom: to cut it down would be a shame and a mistake. The priest – a person of resourceful yet unscientific character – came up with a quick fix: he shall tie one end of a rope to his car, the other to the tree and drive a few meters - causing the young tree to bend backward just enough to liberate the screaming animal onto solid ground. He did as he planned but underestimated the elasticity of the young tree trunk: as he stopped the car just far away enough for Omnibus to leap down, the rope snapped. The tree, in a catapult-like manner, flung backward rapidly, launching poor shrieking Omnibus into an unknown direction far away.

As later discovered in searching for the cat, in one small apartment an interaction between two inhabitants of the village has occurred *the night before*. 9-year-old Masha, having completed her homework and done the chores, knocked on her mother's door ready to pop the big question. Not that she hasn't asked before, but she was always met with "We'll see how your grades are." Well, her grades were now exceptional and so was her behaviour record, so Masha (despite having little confidence in her chances) could not think of a better time to ask. She came in and said: "Mommy, can we *please* finally get a kitten? I promise to look after him and clean his box, I'm doing well in school, and I just really want to have a cat to look after and raise?" The mother sighed: she knew the animal would in the end become her own responsibility and began searching for excuses. The conversation went as follows:

- "It's not a toy."
- "I know that, mommy!"
- "We have little space."
- "But he can live in my room!"
- "Are you sure you are ready to assume responsibility for a living animal?"
- "Yes, I am, mother!"

The child was just not giving in…

- "Okay," said the mother, "we can think about it. Masha, why don't you pray to God for a cat and see what happens? If this be God's will, we will have a cat!"

The conversation ended at that.

The next morning, a Sunday, young Masha was sitting at the kitchen table drawing, her mother was cooking a big bowl of soup. At that moment, ill-fated Omnibus flies right through the kitchen window, gets briefly entangled in the curtain, frees himself and then proceeds to run around the house frantically screaming (all this happens within a matter of a few seconds). The child's mouth opens in disbelief: "It worked! God heard my prayers! We have a cat!" The mother (who was a faithful Christian but had no idea that *this* was how God works) gasps, covers her mouth, and faints, dropping the bowl of soup onto the floor. Curtain call…

If this storyhad not been told through the mouth of that very priest (who, as a faithful man of God, I doubt would tell untruths), I would most probably have dismissed this recital as a fairy-tale. Call it an unbelievable coincidence, a twisted play of circumstance, a glitch in the matrix or simply "God's Will." I call it a miracle because, hey, what are the chances of flinging a cat a few hundred metres and hitting **the** apartment in which a little girl prayed for a cat the night before? Almost zero.

This is a nice little story, one that people may remember, but does it have any relevance whatsoever? Why have I chosen this anecdote to conclude a book about self-realization, financial attainment, and success? Surely, success rarely comes about through miracles! Or am I telling you to "pray" for your "cat" and expect wonders?

Well, there is another kind of miracle. This kind of miracle is not embodied through sole prayer or luck, yet in my eyes is even more "miraculous" than others and is central to unlocking the power of the "Manifesto." Hear this:

Age one to six: raised by her strict grandmother in poverty, wearing potato sacks as dresses and getting beaten so hard she develops scarring on her back. Age seven to 13: endures vicious sexual abuse by the hands of her cousin, uncle, and a family friend in Milwaukee. Age 14: gives birth to a pre-mature baby that dies in hospital only weeks later. Age 19: while attending Tennessee State University, she becomes the youngest news anchor and the only black female news anchor in the state. Age 29: takes over the "AM Chicago" morning talk-show, causing the previously low-rated program to become the highest-rated show in Chicago. Age 32: launches her own, nationwide show which turns into a wild success. Thereafter, she participates in tens of movies and TV-shows, both as an actor and a producer, becomes one of the most respected executives, donates millions to charitable causes, builds a media empire, and amasses a fortune of 2.7 billion dollars. The name? Oprah Winfrey.

This is a miracle. **This** is remarkable. Winfrey does, by the way, believe in God – as a Baptist Christian, she (I'm sure) has prayed tirelessly for her very own "cat." But despite all of the dreadful hardships she had endured, despite the fact that life has had all odds stacked against her, she never sat around as a victim *awaiting* a miracle. Oprah took matters into her own hands, *she made herself* even though social and economic circumstance had clearly set her up for failure (most likely drug abuse, crime, and poverty). **This** is the kind of miracle I'm talking about – a miracle *actively manifested* by its ultimate beneficiary.

I truly do hope none of my readers go through as much difficulty and struggle as Ms Winfrey. I also hope that none of my readers have the audacity to blame their inaction or their current financial state of things "beyond their control." If someone with the story of Oprah can "make it," then sure as hell can you. So often do I hear: "I wasn't born rich, I will not die rich" and "I'm good enough with doing *reasonably* well in life – why bother with risk and hard work to achieve "additional" success?" Get up off the couch and…

Be ambitious. Dream. Project. Develop a passion – this will be the only initial driving force powerful enough to cause you *to act* upon anything you have learned in the "Manifesto." Remember, this book is most valuable as a source of knowledge when it is also seen as a **call to action.** *Get things done!* I have given you many tools and established several steppingstones for you to leap into anything – so say to yourself: "By the end of this year, I will have invested $5000 in stocks" or "The way he described Venture Capital has got me interested – I will look for and secure an internship at a VC firm." There is no such thing as "overly-ambitious" but let's not forget to practice rationality and objectivity in our plans. *Make that promise. Plan that aim. Act on it.* You are the only one who can use this book to change your life for the better.

Hence, yes, miracles do exist, and someone in the world is out there right now being blessed with a metaphorical "cat" for their own prayers. Someone, but not me and you. We are capitalists, we are "doers," we are *active manifesters* – we make our own miracles happen.

So,

Manifest!

List of Sources: Literature, Movies, Websites, and More:

This page contains important information. I advise you to not to skim over this lightly as you will almost certainly *need* to use the recommended resources to help with all your "manifesting." Download those apps. Subscribe to those newspapers. Now.

You may also genuinely *enjoy* the books and movies listed here – though some of them are not directly linked to money or wealth creation, they all will serve an excellent job at expanding both your generic and specific knowledge... and keep you interested!

Let's be real: everyone needs to unwind somehow. Stocks, venture capital, spending habits, mental tricks and other topics mentioned in the "Manifesto" are crucial things, but they cannot possibly consume *all* of your time. To grow by day, one has to rest by night and so I have no expectation of you, the reader (perhaps, inspired by principles of rationality, objectivity and healthy selfishness), to abandon Netflix, YouTube and Instagram for good. This would akin to crash-dieting: you may do well implementing my core ideas for a while but if you never give yourself any slack, you'll burn out quite fast. My point is simple: since you're going to spend time on these platforms anyway, you might as well consume content which is both interesting *and* of use to you in the future. On Netflix, watch Billions over Family Guy or Inbetweeners. On YouTube, watch about how Hyperloop is about to turn the global transport industry upside down, or how China is building an economic "Silk Road" which basically grants it far-reaching economic dominance over most Asian countries... These things matter! They're going on around you, you are affected by them, you can benefit from them or even change them, but not if you're watching "Celebrity Fails" or "Rumours about Cardi B's

Engagement." Very soon, the world won't give a damn about these people, their rumours, their babies and their engagements, and the sizes of their butts. To be a well-prepared and well-positioned citizen of the future, stop consuming time-wasting content and begin consuming reusable, functional, relevant information.

With all of this said, please keep in mind: regardless of how good the quality of your content is, it will amount to no change of your financial status if unbacked by action. The "Manifesto" is a lot to digest, a lot to read up on, and a lot to do. I would consider it completely reasonable to having read this book, give yourself some "learning" time. Perhaps pick up a few of the books I recommended, watch a few movies, and/or read a few sites. Decide what the "Manifesto" can do for you. Consume information. Make a plan. Then dive into action.

Investor / Reader / Businessperson Applications & Sites

- **Yahoo Finance** – *stock prices, company research, portfolio monitoring, news updates. Useful as both an application and (even more so) as a desktop version.*
- **Bloomberg & Terminal** – *Bloomberg itself is useful as a financial news source and stock quotes. It also offers Terminal – a costly yet useful subscription soft and hardware for portfolio management and in-depth financial analysis.*
- **StockMarketEye** – *a great, simple in use Mac/Windows application for monitoring your daily gains and losses and managing your stock / bond / derivatives portfolio. Fantastic for amateurs.*
- **Financial Times, BBC, Business Insider, The Economist, CNN Money, TechCrunch, Seeking Alpha**– *all great news sources to be downloaded on your phone.*
- **eToro** – *a great platform for beginners to dip your feet into water when speculating on stock / bond / FX / other asset prices. Should be used to jumpstart your portfolio before moving on to speak to your bank for more professional brokerage services.*
- **Coinbase, Kraken** – *both trusted cryptocurrency exchange platforms where you can buy a position for as little as 10 dollars.*
- **Coinmarketcap** – *a great app (iOS and Android) for monitoring your cryptocurrency holdings.*

Financial and Business Literature Shortlist:

- *Principles* – *Ray Dalio*
- *Zero to One* – *Peter Thiel*
- *The Purple Cow* – *Seth Godin*
- *Think and Grow Rich* – *Napoleon Hill*
- *What They Don't Teach You at Harvard Business School* – *Mark McCormack*
- *The Intelligent Investor* – *Benjamin Graham*
- *Rich Dad Poor Dad* – *Robert Kiyosaki*
- *The Virgin Way* – *Richard Branson*
- *Steve Jobs* - *Walter Isaacson*
- *The Lean Startup* – *Eric Riles*
- *The 7 Habits of Highly Effective People* – *Stephen Covey*
- *The Richest Man in Babylon* – *George Clason*

Para-Finance / Novels / Educational Literature Shortlist:

- **The Financier, Titan, Stoic (Trilogy)** – *Theodore Dreiser*
- **One Hundred Years of Solitude** – *Gabriel Garcia Markes*
- **Crime and Punishment** – *Feodor Dostoevsky*
- **For Whom the Bell Tolls** – *Ernst Hemingway*
- **The Glass Bead Game** – *Herman Hesse*
- **1984, Animal Farm** – *George Orwell*
- **The Great Gatsby** – *F. Scott Fitzgerald*
- **Vanity Fair** – *William Makepeace Thackeray*
- **The Three Comrades** – *Erich Maria Remark*
- **Pride and Prejudice** – *Jane Austin*
- **Anna Karenina, War and Peace** – *Leo Tolstoy*
- **The Stories** – *Anton Chekhov*
- **Of Mice and Men** – *John Steinbeck*
- **The Catcher in the Rye** - *Jerome Salinger*
- **The International Jew (both vols)** – *Henry Ford*
- **Catch 22** – *Joseph Heller*

Entrepreneur / Finance / Motivational Films Shortlist:

- The Founder
- The Social Network
- The Big Short
- The Wolf of Wall Street
- Bill Gates Netflix Documentary
- Nine Angry Men
- Pursuit of Happiness
- Laundromat
- Thank You for Smoking
- Margin Call
- The Great Hack
- The Start-up Kids
- Something Ventured
- Pirates of the Silicon Valley
- Billions (TV-Series)
- Catch Me If You Can
- Vice (Dick Cheney)

Contact Details (Get in Touch!)

The Team (inquiries, proposals, investment opportunities)
info@capiman.com

Feedback (feedback on the Manifesto, ideas, questions)
feedback@capiman.com

Myself (questions, proposals, advice or all else)
chief@capiman.com and on Instagram: @DIMZ

@DIMZ

Made in the USA
Middletown, DE
18 March 2020